Past Lives and Present Karma

Past Lives and Present Karma

Ann Jaffin

ARE PRESS

ASSOCIATION FOR
RESEARCH AND
ENLIGHTENMENT

A.R.E. Press • Virginia Beach • Virginia

A.R.E. Press
215 67th Street
Virginia Beach, VA 23451-2061

ISBN-13: 978-0-87604-532-9

Cover design by Christine Fulcher

To

Stan—my helpmeet and computer-savvy husband of more than thirty years, for all of the support and opportunities. I couldn't have done it without you.

To Karen, Doug, and Brian Richards—my Virginia Beach family, for their bottomless hospitality, wise counsel, and warm friendship.

To John Van Auken—from whom I've learned much and who first suggested that I write a book.

CONTENTS

Acknowledgments

I want to acknowledge the very special contributions of the following people.

My two lady healers—Dr. Genevieve Haller and Aldona Simanavichus. Genevieve—chiropractor par excellence!—was always there for me. She not only helped to heal me, she loved me. And my very unique medical masseuse, Aldona, has kept my hands open and functional, without which I could not have written this book.

My family—my beloved grandfather and twin soul, Bob, who visited me when his soul departed his body and launched my interest in the mystical. I salute my role model and mother, Ella Taylor, who introduced me to Edgar Cayce in 1967. I also want to express my deep gratitude to my daughter, Roberta Rossi, who was willing to incarnate despite viewing the rough waters of my river of life and at a time when I was very karmically clueless. I am grateful to Bobbi and her husband, Tony, for attracting the souls of my two very dear grandchildren—Jennifer and Jonathan. I want them to know the real me through this book.

I am grateful to three friends who took the time to read my manuscript—Barbara Finch, Kathy Callahan, and Karen Richards. Thanks also to all those who sent me stories to include that demonstrate the practicality of spiritually.

And thanks to Edgar Cayce for his lifetimes of service and to all those who have worked to preserve and disseminate the wisdom found in his readings. I don't know where I would be without them.

Most of all, I want to express my profound gratitude for all the inspiration and encouragement to the Author of all good works and blessings.

Introduction–Clobbered by Karma

We have met the enemy and he is us.—Pogo

Karmically Clueless

. . . if there is trouble in thy mind, in thy body, in thy spirit—or purpose . . . sin lieth at that door.   1537-1

Remember when John Lennon warned us that instant karma was going to get us and knock us off our feet? I feel like he must have been talking to me. I guess you could say in 1967 that I was karmically clueless. I might have heard the word *karma* in our pop culture, but I was a young teacher. I was in love. Life was good. What had karma to do with me? I had no idea that both so-called good karma and bad karma were creeping up on me. I naively thought that together with my young daughter, Bobbi, I could just put my failed, youthful marriage behind me and move on. The past was past and I was moving on. Boy, was I wrong!

Much of my good karma in this lifetime has come through my mother. In 1967 she gave me a gift that would change my life. She handed me a copy of *The Sleeping Prophet*, the bestselling book about Edgar Cayce by Jess Stearn, and said, "I think you might be interested in this." That was putting it mildly; I was immediately and totally enthralled. I can see now that grace in the form of this book entered my life shortly before marital karma walloped me.

I've always wanted to know the answers to the great questions in life: Who am I? What am I doing here? What happens when we die? What is God? To borrow a quote from Dr. Raymond Moody, pioneer in investigating near-death experiences, "I guess I was born with congenital philosophitis." Over the years, I have found, by far, the most satisfying answers to these and other eternal questions in the Cayce readings. But in 1967 I had no idea that I was soon to be broadsided by instant karma in the form of my second husband. I also had no idea how very hard the next few years would be or how the Cayce readings would give me a new lease on life when I desperately needed it. Most importantly, it would be many years before I understood from Cayce that karma, no matter how painful, can be transformed into grace.

So in 1967 I charged headlong into a second youthful marriage with a man who, like me, had just gotten a divorce. The relationship quickly began to sour. Ever in denial, after teaching for a couple of years, I gave up my teaching job and we moved to the country to restore a pre-Civil War house.

In 1971 it all fell apart. Early in the new year, my husband told me that he wanted a divorce! Talk about clueless, I could not have been more stunned. He soon abandoned me and my daughter, and although I was not yet thirty years old, I was convinced that my life was over. This was at a time when multiple divorce was not yet common. I felt like a complete and utter failure, unable to trust my own judgment. I had no real job—only a mountain of debt. My daughter was traumatized, but she was also my anchor. Only her needs kept me putting one foot in front of the other.

Even in my dazed state, it didn't take long for me to begin to realize that I had been clobbered by karma. In a reading given in 1942, Cayce had told a young woman: "Here, with this individual, ye have some karma (as some people call) to be worked out; for ye did not always agree. But as husband and wife would be a hard way to meet same!" (2582-3) Just to be sure that I didn't miss the point, this reading was given on my birthday—September 10! I had to accept responsibility—I had brought it on myself. My life was in shambles. Like many people, I found out the hard way that there is no better course correction than deep pain. But, years later, I was very glad that I had the strength to move through this instant karma in a few years rather than carrying it into another lifetime.

Parental Relationships

Be ye unhurt by hard words.   *262-83*

Nineteen seventy-five was a major turning point in my life. Hoping that I had evened out my marital karma, I married Stan, my present husband, after a courtship of nearly four years. Having been single and married more often than most people, I knew that I preferred to be married. I also knew Cayce had told a forty-nine-year-old woman that "it is well for the entity to be wedded—this is the natural life of an individual entity in the earth." (3379-2)

However, to my consternation, within a couple weeks of our marriage, my father, with whom I had never gotten along, and my paternal grandmother, who had helped to raise me, moved back into our area. Much later, when I delved into some of my past lives through hypnotic regression, I found that my father had murdered me in a key past life! I was now facing one of the most difficult karmic situations of my life. But first, a little background.

The contrast in my parents was overwhelming—maybe a case of opposites attract. For example, years later when I first told my elderly mother that she needed to move from an independent apartment into an assisted living apartment, she was resistant. After thinking about it for a few minutes, she asked me, "Will it make it easier on you?" When I said, "Yes," she said, "Then I'll do it." As usual, Mom was putting me first. In stark contrast, my father once told me, "I hope you die before I do so I can spit on your grave!" Nice guy. A cardinal principle in the Cayce readings is balance. I guess my parents kind of balanced each other out.

These relationships were no accidents. Whether we want to hear it or not, Cayce tells us that we choose our parents:

(Q) For what purpose did I choose my particular parents at this time?
(A) The help that they may give, and the help *ye* may give.

1442-1

(Q) For what purpose did I choose my present parents in this incarnation?
(A) For thine own enlightenment, and thy parents' understanding.

2632-1

Looking back, I can now see that grace entered my life in a form that reminds me of Cayce's description of the three dimensions of the Earth—time, space, and patience. Time, in that my parents' marriage was, not surprisingly, very brief. Space, in that my father quickly remarried and moved out of state. Patience, in the form of grandparents who took care of me while mom worked, and loved me like their own.

But it all came home to roost in 1975, shortly after Stan and I were married. My father's second wife left him, and he and my paternal grandmother moved nearby. I had inherited a neuromuscular disease from my father, and since he did not take good care of himself, he was failing fast. He decided that he and Grandma should move in with us! Since I definitely did not want a third divorce, push came to shove. Ironically, they wound up moving in with my first husband and *his* second wife! My father then promptly disinherited me in their favor. I chose not to pursue the issue in court and have never regretted that decision. Again, karma seemed to be the best explanation for this bizarre situation.

The sharp response that Cayce had given to a father who asked about his past-life relationship with his handicapped daughter kept me trying to work constructively with my family situation: "In the experience before this you could have helped and didn't. You'd better help in the present." (3581-1)

So, despite hard feelings all around, I continued to try to help my father and grandmother, especially after they were relieved of their money and dumped into nursing homes. With my increasing belief in reincarnation, I steeled myself with the not very altruistic thought that

I did not want to do this over again in another lifetime. I wanted to clear up what I could right now. Cayce could not have made it plainer: "No problem may be run away from. *Meet* it *now!*" (1204-3)

Hereditary Illness

. . . weaknesses in the flesh are the scars of the soul!   275-19

I had been diagnosed at the National Institutes of Health (NIH) with Charcot–Marie–Tooth (CMT) disease in 1965 while I was still in college. CMT is an incurable, progressive, hereditary, neuromuscular condition that affects the limbs. Since the disease didn't bother me much at that time and NIH had no cure or treatment to recommend, in a state of youthful denial, I just ignored it for twenty years.

Frankly, my father's death in 1982 was a relief. But seeing his physical decline had frightened me. When I saw how wasted his leg muscles had become, I knew I needed to do something. The big question was, What could I do? My visit to Johns Hopkins' neuromuscular clinic in May 1983 is seared into my memory. After painful diagnostic tests, the head of this prestigious clinic told me that he thought that I would wind up in leg braces like my father. I sat there with tears streaming down my face and thought defiantly, "Not me, buddy, because I know about Edgar Cayce!"

Thankfully, through my involvement with the Association for Research and Enlightenment (A.R.E., the Edgar Cayce organization), I knew where to look. As I began to seek, grace appeared in the form of an article in the *A.R.E. Journal*, predecessor to *Venture Inward* magazine. I was thrilled when I saw an article on Charcot–Marie–Tooth disease written by a Virginia Beach chiropractor, Dr. Genevieve Haller. The article described Dr. Haller's promising work with a woman a little older than I was whose CMT required her to use a crutch to walk. Dr. Haller had used Cayce's broad-based holistic approach, employing many different therapies over several years. The patient had improved enough to work part-time and resume driving her car! Later, I had a chance to talk with this lady, and she told me that when she started working with Dr. Haller, she was so weak that she needed help just to go to the store. A few years later, she was strong enough to go back to school.

I felt guided and blessed when Dr. Haller asked me to become the pilot patient in a new program called a "holistic clinic without walls," which she and several associates launched in the fall of 1983. I worked intensively with therapies that Edgar Cayce had recommended for neuromuscular diseases, especially a device that he had invented called the wet-cell battery. As far as I know, Dr. Haller's other patient and I are the only people with CMT who have ever reported improvement. Five years later, NIH was able to record improved nerve conductivity in my limbs! This was supposed to be impossible. But again, I knew that Cayce had said, "There are in truth no incurable conditions . . . " (3744-2)

I had some obvious clues that this condition was karmic: First, I had inherited the disease from my father, with whom I had a very prickly relationship. Second and synchronistically, not only was the middle name of the disease the same as my middle name, the middle name of Dr. Haller's other CMT patient was also Marie. Talk about something having your name on it!

In many respects, working with Dr. Haller was a major turning point for me. I had to make a firm commitment to make changes in my life if I wanted to continue walking unaided. I needed to bring my life into better balance to promote healing. Most of all, I knew that I was "meeting self," in the parlance of the Cayce readings.

With my interest in reincarnation, I wanted to find out where this hereditary condition had originated. Where else could one look for the cause of an inborn illness but in a past life? In 1984 I made an appointment for hypnotic regression with Carolyn Gelone, who was recommended by Dr. Haller. The information, which I will share later, that poured out of my unconscious mind provided a tumultuous fount of rich insights into both the health and the relationship karma that I was encountering in my present life. It provided vivid answers to anguished questions that I, like so many others, have asked: Why me? Why did this have to happen to me? What have I done to deserve this?

All of this further stimulated me to make a deeper study of the Cayce readings on reincarnation and karma and to look for guidance on how to heal my body and my relationships. The results of this search sustained me when I was diagnosed with Dupuytren's disease in 1991. This second hereditary condition, which also affects the limbs, had come through my mother's side of the family. But now I was able to recognize that this was another opportunity to learn some additional karmic lessons in my present life. I also knew that Cayce had put it this way:

> **Karma is cause oft of hereditary conditions so called. Then indeed does the soul inherit that it has builded in its experience with its fellow man in material relationships.** 3313-1

This path of pain and self-discovery also led me to write this book—to share what I have found helpful in moving from past problems to present solutions.

Part I:
Reincarnation and Interplanetary Sojourns

No entity enters a material sojourn by chance, but from those realms of consciousness in which it has dwelt during the interims between earthly sojourns, the entity chooses that environ through which it may make manifest those corrections—or those choices it has made and does make in its real or in its inner self.   3027-2

Hence there are urges, or influences—not as astrological aspects but from sojourns through which the entity has passed—or experiences during the interims between earthly manifestations. These become manifested in the dreams, the hopes; while the earthly sojourns find expression in the emotions of the body; and not because a star, a constellation, or even any phase of the zodiac sign, was in such and such a position at the time of birth . . .

    Thus these, in the deeper sense, have that same influence from astrological sojourns ye have as the hereditary forces, or that deep in the inner being; while the material or earthly sojourns influence the deeper environmental forces.   2549-1

1

Reincarnation–Another Chance to Get It Right

Be ye ... perfect, even as your Father ... in heaven is perfect.

Matthew 5:48

Edgar Cayce's Big Surprise

The purpose of each soul's manifestation is to be not only good but good for something.   843-3

Surely, it was one of the greatest shocks of Edgar Cayce's life when he found he had told Arthur Lammers in a 1923 reading that this was Lammers' third lifetime and that he had once been a monk. (5717-1) Actually, Cayce's source gave this same information twice, in Lammers' first and second life readings, one week apart. (5717-1 and -2) Moreover, in a physical reading that Cayce gave for himself two days after Lammers' second reading, the Source told Cayce that he (Cayce) had lived seven lifetimes in the Earth! (294-7) It was bad enough that the value of astrology had already been confirmed by a reading in 1919 (254-2), but reincarnation was far worse. The idea seemed to contradict the traditional Christian faith which Edgar and his wife Gertrude held so very dear and which was the foundation of their lives.

Characteristically, Edgar turned to his worn and trusty Bible to search for answers about this new and troubling concept. Although the actual words *reincarnation* and *karma* are not found in our modern Bibles, Cayce found that these concepts are certainly implied in many passages in both the Old and New Testaments. Indeed, the concepts of reincarnation and karma not only make some passages more understandable, they seem to offer the only reasonable explanation at times. After searching the Scriptures and praying for guidance, Edgar concluded, "I can read reincarnation into the Bible—and you can read it right out again!"[1]

It took a couple of weeks, but on November 7, 1923, Cayce finally agreed to ask about his prior associations with Lammers and two other business associates, and the past–life information poured out. (5717-5) The Source identified several previous lives for each man. There was no turning back.

It seems as if the Source knew that the time was now ripe and that Edgar was ready to grapple with this new and challenging concept. Arthur Lammers' interest in astrology and reincarnation had doubtlessly helped to pave the way for this breakthrough. And, finally, after years of struggling to find a secretary who was not only skilled enough but also unflappable enough to take down the readings, Gladys Davis had been hired on August 30. Gladys, who would later be told in a life reading that she was Edgar's twin soul, had again incarnated with him, to fulfill a critical role as his devoted, lifelong secretary, preserving most of the more than fourteen thousand readings for posterity. The stage was now set for the readings to grow beyond the physical and into the spiritual realms. In retrospect, it seems clear that the Source had a deeper purpose and broader vision of how this unique work was to be of service to humanity.

Why Are We Here?

Each soul that enters the material manifestation has something to contribute . . .   1350-1

The two thousand life readings that deal with reincarnation and karma provide many fascinating insights that help us to understand more about how these great, universal laws actually work. According to

Cayce, we have been in the Earth for more than 10.5 million years. Once having become stuck here in karma, which we might call being "karmalized," we must now get unstuck and work our way out, no matter how long it takes. From the perspective of the readings, it is clear that the only pathway out is through many lifetimes in which we can grow toward the perfection that is our ultimate destiny. Our beautiful little planet is a very sticky place.

Although we can't get a reading from Edgar Cayce today, we can still learn a great deal from the questions that people asked in their readings. A frequently asked question concerned one's purposes for reincarnating. Cayce often indicated that some of these reasons are universal and apply to all of us.

> (Q) What is the work God wants me to do while here on Earth?
> (A) That you do and say to the glory of God and not to [3356] or any other individual! The whole purpose of a soul in the earth is to glorify the Creative Forces . . .   3356-1

> (Q) What is my specific mission and objective in this material incarnation? . . .
> (A) The activities of an individual entity through any given experience are to make the paths straight. Where there have been the misapplication, mis-conception of the activities of Creative Forces in an individual experience, then it is the correcting of same.   877-22

> (Q) For what did I come into this plane at this time?
> (A) To meet self; for thou hast walked backwards . . . Go *forward!* Ever . . . is the command of Creative Force to "*Go forward!*"
>   1094-1

In 1942 a stenographer was given encouragement and advice that we should all strive to remember. Soul growth can come through attending to the little things that are right in front of us.

> . . . ye came for a definite purpose. Each soul . . . has a definite

job to do. But ye alone may find and do that job!

Then do with thy might what thy hands find to do day by day, being not unmindful that though it may appear to be the more menial job, in same ye may find thine own soul shining through!

2823-1

The readings consistently teach that our universe is both lawful and purposeful. To have another chance at life is a high privilege as well as a great responsibility.

(Q) Is there anything in particular I can do now to accomplish the reason for present incarnation?

(A) If there hadn't been you wouldn't be allowed to be in the earth in the present! . . .   3051-7

How Often Do We Reincarnate?

The soul . . . only enter[s] matter, or a new house, in incarnations.

1494-1

People often wonder about the number of lifetimes they have lived and how long this whole process will take. The readings give no rule governing the number of incarnations. It's up to us—how long will we take to meet our karma and move into grace?

In a physical reading that Cayce gave for himself in 1923, the Source came straight out and told him that he had lived seven lifetimes in the Earth. (294-7) As we saw, Arthur Lammers had been told that this was his "third appearance on this plane" (5717-1), and George Klingensmith, another business associate, was told that he had "been four times upon this earth plane." (4121-1)

In June of 1944 a thirty-eight-year-old freight agent asked Cayce, "When and where will I next incarnate and will I be associated with associates of this incarnation and whom?" Cayce's response was somewhat sobering:

Better get into shape so that you can incarnate. That depends a great deal upon what one does about the present opportunities.

It isn't set for time immemorial as to be what you will be from one experience to the other. For, as has been given, there are unchangeable laws. The Creator intended man to be a companion with Him. Whether in heaven or in the earth or in whatever consciousness, a companion with the Creator. How many will it require for thee to be able to be a companion with the Creative Forces where ever you are? That is also a law. What ye sow, ye reap. 416-18

Do We Change Sex From One Incarnation to Another?

. . . sex change is more from desire than from physical *earth incarnation's influence—see?* 311-3

In March 1929, Morton Blumenthal, one of Cayce's greatest benefactors, asked how we change sex in different incarnations.

How oft has there been the expression heard, "Were I a man—" or "Were I a woman—I would do so and so?" They do it! That as is constantly builded in the mental being takes shape in the home of the soul, whether to build that of the man or woman in a material world . . . and as these forces then are builded, they take physical form through that experienced by . . . the soul. The soul is that everlasting portion of a body that is either crowded into that (beings that are known as men and women) of small or great stature. 900-429

Through desire, then, we build our future body as a man or a woman with the power of our mind.

Two years later, another man asked Cayce the same question:

(Q) What causes changes in sex and why do some change, others not?
(A) That is from the *spiritual* desire . . . one may appear in the earth as male or female as a regular or at intervals, according to the *development*. 311-3

Again Cayce affirms that our desires build the sex of our future bodies. The sex of the body is just one of the choices that the soul must make when it reincarnates. The key issue that ultimately determines our sex, or even our race or color, is in what form our soul can best develop spiritually in its next experience.

> As to race, color or sex—this depends upon that experience necessary for the completion, for the building up of the purposes for which each and every soul manifests in the material experience.   294-189

How Long Is the Interval Between Lives?

> *. . . how much greater is a day in the house of the Lord—or a moment in His presence—than a thousand years in carnal forces?*
> *262-57*

Because life in the Earth is so very challenging, the Cayce readings state that the longer the time period that we spend out of the Earth in the nonphysical dimensions between lifetimes, the greater our progress tends to be. Souls who rush back to reincarnate quickly are usually making it more difficult on themselves.

> For oft, the longer the periods between the earthly sojourns the greater has been — or may be — the development of the soul entity to that which *each* soul *is* to attain through its appearances among men.   1486-1

Apparently, there are no general rules about the length of the interval between lifetimes. However, we can glimpse some of the factors that bear on this question. A young student asked why her soul had waited "until this incarnation to make good karma from the Roman period?" Cayce responded, "Because it couldn't do it before!" (275–25) Perhaps her soul was not ready, or perhaps the circumstances were not right until that time. Perhaps the various souls that she could best interact with were not incarnate until then. The soul has free will, and cause and effect is always operative. In its desire for growth, the soul makes decisions based upon many karmic factors that are unknowable to us in third-dimensional consciousness.

When Edgar asked about his next incarnation, he was told:

> As to when—it may be perhaps a hundred, two hundred, three hundred, a thousand years—as you may count time in the present. This may not be given. For how gave He? The day no man knoweth, *only* the Father in heaven knoweth it . . .
>
> 294-189

Soul Groups and Reincarnation Cycles

And remember you'll be back again!   4047-1

The readings indicate that our souls often reincarnate in groups and cycle together in both our physical and nonphysical experiences. We focus and work on our own individual soul purpose and lessons in the different dimensions. In addition, groups of souls cycle in and out of the Earth together time and again to work on shared issues and challenges for the betterment of all those involved. A very interesting soul group, which included Edgar Cayce and many of his associates, had been a part of two great, ancient civilizations—Atlantis and Egypt. These powerful souls profoundly impacted our world in ancient times and again during the twentieth century.

> As so oft indicated, in periods certain individuals or groups of souls enter. As, between '09 and '12 . . . brought that great influx of Atlanteans that have had and are having such an influence in the affairs of the world today. Not a hero in this present war that was not an Atlantean as yet, living or dead!   3029-1

The readings warned in 1934 that the incoming Atlanteans could have a very positive or a very negative influence on our world. They were described as wily souls with high mental abilities and given to "such an engorgement of the carnal influences." Because of "self-indulgences by so many in . . . Atlantis . . . *these* souls may rule or ruin man's association in the earth during their sojourn in the present." (518-1)

The following reading posed a very sobering and still very timely question about these Atlanteans:

> . . . is it any wonder that—if they made such alterations in the affairs of the earth in their day, as to bring destruction upon themselves—if they are entering now, they might make many changes in the affairs of peoples and individuals in the present?
> 364-1

When Cayce was asked about his associates who had past lives in Egypt, the reading said that these "would run into many, many numbers" and that "again the cycle has rolled to that period when the individual entities again in the earth's experience gather together for a definite work . . ." (254-47) Apparently, many souls from ancient Egypt, including all the members of Edgar's immediate family, had purposefully incarnated together again to continue this spiritual work, which had begun in these earlier times.

Another soul group cycling together for a particular purpose caught my eye because I was born during the period that Cayce mentions:

> . . . those entering the material plane in '43, '44, '45, '46 are purposeful individual entities, and much will depend upon these souls as to what manner of activity will be in the world a score of years hence.
> 5306-1

> For, as will be seen in not too distant a future, all those souls that enter the material plane through the period of '43, '44 and '45 will apparently be destined to fulfil interesting roles in their service to their fellow man, and find a very unusual approach to same.
> 2892-2

Why Don't We Remember Our Past Lives?

Ye only became aware of same as it became necessary for its practical application in [your] experience!   *2301-4*

A commonly asked question is, Why don't we remember our past lives? The answer is in part that neither our physical bodies nor our conscious minds reincarnate. These two vessels are created anew each lifetime, so we don't remember the last life we lived in the same way that we remember the last meal we ate. It is our soul and our higher mind which are eternal and immortal and which reincarnate. They contain total memory of all we are and all we have done since we were first created—a humbling thought indeed.

Cayce compares remembering past lives to learning lessons when we were in school. Although we don't remember all the details of our school instruction as we move through life, our schooling creates a mental context that is helpful when we address problems in our daily lives.

> One may ask, ... *Why*, then, does one not recall more often [past-life] experiences?
> The same may be asked of why there is not the remembering of the time when two and two to the entity became four, or when C A T spelled cat. It always did! Ye only became aware of same as it became necessary for its practical application in [your] experience!   2301-4

So it is with past–life experiences. When it is necessary to make current decisions, past learning, which we do not even remember, helps us deal with present problems. Perhaps it is best not to know all of our past lives and their endless and often sad details. We could become overwhelmed with lost opportunities and regrets. When we study the frequently destructive history of mankind in the Earth and stop to realize that we were participants, we can appreciate the wisdom and grace of this reading:

> As to the experiences in the earth, these have been many and quite varied. Many of these are not well even to be known to self, and thus have they been blotted from the book of thy remembrance, even as He blots them from the book of God's remembrance, if ye love one another, if ye mete to thy fellow man, yea, to thy sisters in all walks of experience, that love of which ye are capable in thine self. For he who hath loved much, to that

one may much be given.   5231-1

Do Animals Reincarnate?

But ask the beasts, and they shall teach thee . . . Job 12:7

The Cayce readings seem to tell us that animals may travel with us from one lifetime to another. Although there is not much information about this subject in the readings, what is there is fascinating. Most of what we find in the Cayce readings about the reincarnation of animals we owe to Mrs. [268]. When this lady asked about her past–life relationship with her niece, Cayce told her that they had been together in a Roman experience. The woman then asked about a possible past life with her little dog, Mona. Cayce calmly replied, "In the same experience." Wanting to be certain that she understood, she asked, "In the Roman?" Cayce confirmed it and replied, "The Roman." She followed up by asking, "Was she a dog then?" Doubtlessly to the amazement of all, Cayce said that the dog had been "a lion!" (268-3)

A week later, Mrs. [268] got a reading for her husband and asked about his past relationship to Mona:

(Q) What relation is he to the little dog Mona?
(A) He fought with the body in the Roman experience.
(Q) What was Mona then?
(A) The lioness that fought with the entity, and with those that destroyed many that the entity was then seeking to aid.   280-1

This information must have generated quite a bit of interest, because other family members also asked about Mona in their readings. The woman's niece asked:

(Q) Will Mona always be a dog?
(A) That depends upon the environ and the surroundings. No.
                                                        405-1

Mrs. [268]'s nephew also got a reading and asked about Mona:

(Q) Could a life reading be obtained through these sources for Aunt [268]'s little dog Mona?
(A) May be. As to *what* it may be is different! It may not be understood, unless you learn dog language!   406-1

As fascinating as all of this is, in some respects, it raises more questions than it answers. Nevertheless, what it tells us adds a new dimension to our understanding not only of reincarnation but of life. The first surprise is that, according to Cayce, Mona reincarnated. She lived in Roman times, and she came back in twentieth-century America. That is surprising enough. But the reading also says that Mona changed form. Although she remained an animal, she had presumably progressed from being a dangerous animal of prey to being a pet. How or why this change occurred, we are not told. She remained female but reincarnated in a much smaller body. The husband's reading provides some clarification that in Rome as a lioness, Mona had fought with him and others that he was trying to help. This certainly sounds like the persecution of Christians, possibly in the Coliseum.

In the niece's reading, we continue to receive startling information about how animals reincarnate. This girl asked a wonderful question about whether Mona would always be a dog. After stating that this depends on the environment and the surroundings, Cayce said, "No," that Mona would not always be a dog. Since there is no more information on Mona's other lifetimes or whether or not animals experience interplanetary sojourns between Earth lives like we do, we can only speculate about these possibilities. How this transformation occurred from wild beast to household pet is not explained, but I think that this is in keeping with Cayce's philosophy of growth and progress for all.

The nephew also asked a clever question in his reading, and Cayce gave another illuminating response. When the boy asked about the possibility of getting a life reading for Mona, Cayce said that although it could be done, no one would understand it unless one learned dog language, clearly implying that dog language exists. Needless to say, no one pursued this idea any further.

Why Study Reincarnation?

*... there is as much reason to dwell upon the thought from whence
the soul came, as it is upon whence the soul goeth.*   3003-1

Some people may ask why it is important to study reincarnation.
Cayce often tells us that understanding our past problems helps us to
cope with our present lives:

> Know that the knowledge of from whence ye came, and your trials
> through those experiences, is as necessary in meeting the every-
> day experiences of life in the Now (for it is ever the Now), as it is
> to study about wither thou wilt go.   342-1

In December of 1938, Cayce warned a fifty-two-year-old businesswoman:

> Too easily does man—with the comforts of the body, with the
> gratifying of appetites—forget that from whence he came and
> whither he goeth—and only the material manifestation is seen or
> sought.   1765-2

The readings assure us that we retain talents from our past-life efforts, which can also serve us well in the present if we look for them. As
the anonymous saying goes, We are our own archaeological digs.

> Has it not been indicated that those who are trained in the former
> experiences in the earth, though they may not have applied the
> principles in the immediate present, may have the wisdom of the
> ages at their disposal—if there is the beginning and the applica-
> tion of self in those directions?   903-33

The Cayce readings count it not only a constructive experience but a
privilege to view our soul's record. It is a unique mental and spiritual
mirror of ourselves:

> For to read, to interpret one's book of remembrance is to help, to
> become a constructive experience. For to know same is to turn to

that as He, the Master, hath given: "Abide in the faith in me and
I will bring to your remembrance all things from the foundations
of the world."

Then, it becomes not only a privilege, not only an opportunity
for one to look into that which has been the accomplishment of
self. For it is indeed not as a mirror that reflects only that which
is before same, but rather it is the mental and spiritual mirror that
becomes a helpful force if it is but applied in constructive ways
and manners in the experience.   1404-1

Therefore, studying reincarnation is really very practical. It not only
helps us to understand ourselves, it helps us to function more effec-
tively as we confront the challenges of our daily life.

2

Attending Planetary College Between Lifetimes

. . . astrological influences are effective in the experience of each and every entity.
398-2

A key concept stressed in the Cayce readings is that life is continuous. It does not end, nor does it stop and start. Despite the outward physical appearance of bodily death and physical disintegration, the essential part of us—our soul—lives on. Because the soul is a part of God, it is indestructible. It is truly eternal.

> Life is a stream, not that which is static or that [which] is here a little and there a little—but is continuous; and is the manifestation of that force we worship as God . . .
> **2549-1**

If life is truly continuous and reincarnation is a fact, the question then arises, Where does our soul go, and what does our soul do between its incarnations on Earth? The Cayce readings provide a unique and fascinating answer to this frequently overlooked question. The readings liken our solar system to a kind of university, comprised of various colleges that present continuing educational opportunities between physical incarnations. When not encased in flesh bodies on Earth, our souls attend the planetary colleges in our solar system! But let's be very clear about this—Cayce is *not* saying that we go physically to these planets or that there is physical life as we know it on Mars, Venus, Jupiter, and so on:

> Not that Venus, Jupiter, Mars, Uranus or any of the planets about this earth's sun have beings or bodies such as are known in the earth's sojourns; but that are peculiar to their own realm . . .
>
>   541-1

> Then there are the sojourns in other realms of the solar system which represent certain attributes. Not that ye maintain a physical earth-body in Mercury, Venus, Jupiter, Uranus or Saturn; but there is an awareness or a consciousness in those realms when absent from the body, and the response to the position those planets occupy in this solar system.   2823-1

> Thus as the soul passes from the aspects about the material environs, or the earth, we find the astrological aspects are represented as stages of consciousness; given names that represent planets or centers or crystallized activity.
>
> Not that flesh and blood, as known in the earth, dwells therein; but in the consciousness, with the form and manner as befits the environ.   1650-1

Cayce's View of Astrology

The strongest power in the destiny of man is the Sun, first; then the closer planets, or those that are coming in ascendency at the time of the birth of the individual . . .   *254-2*

Therefore, astrology, as popularly used and understood, does not represent the full picture, according to Cayce. Heavenly bodies influence us not because of their locations when we are born, but because of our nonphysical experiences literally in the environs and dimensions of those heavenly bodies. Like the concept of reincarnation, this idea com-

ing through the readings must have been another eye-opener to Edgar
and his associates.

> The astrological influences are not because of certain positions
> of the stars or planets, or this or that phase of the astronomical
> signs, but because of the sojourns of the entity there during the
> interims between the earthly appearances.   1681-1

> Thus there are latent urges that arise [within us]; not merely
> because the sun, the moon or the planets are at a certain position
> at the time or place . . . Thus urges astrologically, that have to do
> with the spiritual consciousness are not altogether in keeping
> with the influences commonly accredited to astrology; but [are]
> because of an entity's consciousness in that environ . . . during the
> interims between material entrances or manifestations . . .
>   2988-2

What the Planets Teach Us

*. . . remember . . . the sun, the moon, the planets—have their march-
ing orders from the divine . . .*   *5757-1*

Cayce said that the planetary dimensions are at higher levels than
our earthly three dimensions and are designed for soul instruction in a
way that is difficult for our three-dimensional minds to grasp. "Thus we
find that the sojourns have their direct influence upon the entity . . .
from visions, from that not capable of being expressed in the material—
and words only confuse." (2428-1) Apparently, such communication
problems are not restricted to the Earth.

> (Q) Have I had an incarnation on the planet Jupiter?
> (A) In that environ, yes.
> (Q) Is it possible to secure a reading regarding conditions and my
> sojourn, if any, on that planet?
> (A) If you can understand Jupiterian environs and languages, yes.
>   826-8

In general, Cayce listed four to six planets as influencing a person's present life. However, the planet that most influences a soul is the one from which it departed before reincarnating on Earth. Conversely, how a person lives his or her earthly life, including all the choices made, dictates to what planets the soul goes after death.

> (Q) Explain how . . . planets influence an individual at birth?
> (A) As the entity is born into the earth's plane, the relation to that planet, or that sphere, from which the spirit entity took its flight . . . to enter the earth plane, has the greater influence in the earth's plane. Just as the life lived in the earth's plane directs to what position the spirit entity takes in the spheres.   900-24

The relationship between our earthly incarnations and our planetary sojourns receives some additional clarification in this reading:

> Considering then life, a soul, an entity as a continuous stream of experience—and the activities in the earth's plane as a lesson that is learned by the entity—the experiences through the astrological sojourns become rather as a digesting or an assimilating of that which has been experienced or gained in the lesson.
>   Hence we find these experiences ever being weighed and paralleled with the Creative Forces . . .   1230-1

While we are in a nonphysical state during our sojourns, we internalize our earthly lessons. Using our minds and souls, we assess our progress and evaluate our actions against the highest spiritual standards. In contrast, our earthly manifestations are to "practicalize or materialize" our astrological experiences. (1293-1) We literally come down to Earth to practice and perfect our lessons in the flesh.

Since most of the life readings not only contain information about the person's most relevant past lives but their interim nonphysical experiences as well, there are some fascinating descriptions of the curricula of our planetary colleges.

The high mental abilities . . . come from the Mercurian sojourn . . .

From Venus we find the high regard for duties [and] obligations...Beauty...and art, and all things pertaining to harmony,
arise from the experiences of the entity in those environs . . .

The influence from Jupiter we find making for a universal
appeal, and those things that would have an influence upon
many peoples rather than the individual. Obligations and duties
belong to the individual . . . while the work and the service and
the activities belong to the universe. All of these as we find are
from the Jupiterian sojourn . . .

We find the Uranian experience gives the influences for the
extremes... [as well as an interest] in the occult or psychic nature,
or the mystic nature.   1681-1

As in Mercury pertaining of Mind.
In Mars of Madness.
In Earth as of Flesh.
In Venus as Love.
In Jupiter as Strength.
In Saturn as the beginning of earthly woes, that to which all
insufficient matter is cast for the [new] beginning.
In that of Uranus as of the Psychic.
In that of Neptune as of Mystic.
In Septimus as of Consciousness.
In Arcturus as of the developing.   900-10

Before Pluto was discovered in 1930, Cayce used the name Septimus
for that body, perhaps because it is the seventh planet away from the
Earth. In readings after 1930, Cayce began using the name Pluto.

Most of the qualities ascribed to the planets by Cayce are not at great
variance with modern astrology. However, the exception is Saturn. In
the reading above, Cayce describes Saturn in very sobering terms. It
sounds like the recycling center of our solar system. But Saturn can also
be viewed as grace to a soul who needs a fresh start.

In Saturn we find the sudden or violent changes...And yet these
are testing periods of thy endurance, of thy patience, of thy love

> of truth, harmony and the spirit that faileth not.   1981-1

> From Saturn we find the tendency for the starting of new
> experiences . . .   361-4

The unique vibration of each planet affects the soul and provides an
opportunity for its further development.

> Each planetary influence vibrates at a different rate of vibration.
> An entity entering that influence enters that vibration; [it is] not
> necessary that he change, but it is the grace of God that he may!
> It is part of the universal consciousness, the universal law.
>   281-55

The Special Role of the Earth

> *. . . [earthly] sojourns are as lessons, as grades . . .*   *3226-1*

As most of us have probably learned by now, Earth is an especially
challenging dimension. We might call it the college of hard knocks.
Cayce tells us that our Earth is just what every student loves—a place of
testing. For it is in the earthly plane that we concretely manifest our
true level of consciousness.

> Then, in the many stages of development . . . in the great system
> of the universal forces, and each stage of development made
> manifest through flesh, which is the testing portion of the
> universal vibration. In this manner then, and for this reason, all
> made manifest in flesh . . . [develop] . . . through the eons of time,
> space and *called* eternity.   900-16

The readings make an interesting distinction between how lessons
from past earthly incarnations and lessons from interim planetary experiences influence our present lives. We are told that our emotions
come to us from our past lives in the Earth, and our innate, or inborn, urges
and longings come from our interplanetary sojourns. Even our intuition and our mental abilities come from these nonphysical experiences.

These arise as influences, the emotions from sojourns in the earth and the innate influences from the sojourns in the environs about the earth during the interims between earthly incarnations.

1523-4

Hence we find astrological as well as material sojourns having an influence. The astrological influences are upon the mental or the intuitive forces . . .

These come then as dreams, as visions—not as dreams from the separation of the body, but day dreams and visions in the meditative experiences of the entity.

On the other hand, the material sojourns find greater expression in the emotional forces and influences in the entity's experience. 1681-1

Despite all the influences that we accumulate from our eons on Earth and in the dimensions of planetary consciousness, the Cayce readings never fail to stress the primacy of our will. No influence whatsoever can override our God-given free will. When we make the choice to set an ideal, or standard of behavior, and as the reading below states, have the courage to hold to that ideal in our daily lives, it literally makes the difference between happiness and unhappiness for us.

. . . the earthly sojourn urges are to the emotions, while the mental or innate urges are from the experiences of the soul in the environs about the earth.

But these are merely urges or inclinations, not impelling forces, and these [may be] used . . . as warnings, or as those things to embrace, [and] may be applied in the experience for helpful forces and influences.

Know, however, that it is what the will does about that which is set as its ideal in a mental, in a material or in the physical experiences as well as the spiritual—and then having the courage to carry out that ideal—[which] makes the difference between the constructive and creative forces or relationships and those that make one become rather as a drifter or a ne'er-do-well, or one very unstable and unhappy.   1401-1

Our power as free-willed souls is so unimaginably great that the readings also tell us that not only do the heavenly bodies influence us, we influence them. When giving a discourse on sunspots in 1940, Cayce made these comments:

> . . . do ye wonder then that there become reflected upon even the face of the sun those turmoils and strifes that have been and that are the sin of man?
>
> These become, then, as the influences that would show man as to his littleness in even entertaining hate, injustice, or that which would make a lie. . .
>
> For, as ye do it unto the least, ye do it unto the Maker—even as to the sun which reflects those turmoils that arise with thee; even as the earthquake, even as wars and hates, even as the influences in thy life day by day.
>
> Then, what are the sunspots? A natural consequence of that turmoil which the sons of God in the earth reflect upon same.
>
>   5757-1

As spiritual creations, our power knows no bounds!

3

Heredity–We Are Our Own Ancestors

You have inherited most from yourself, not from family!   1233-1

As the bearer of two hereditary diseases and a believer in reincarnation, I first used hypnotic regression to look for the roots of these conditions in past lives. What I discovered there was illuminating and very thought-provoking—I'll share some highlights in chapter 9. But as a student of the Edgar Cayce readings, I knew that there was more to the story. I knew that I needed to look beyond the physical to the roles of the mind and the spirit.

First, ours is a lawful universe, always. As Cayce's tone emphasized, *"Like begets like!"* (262-82) Doing good leads to so-called good karma. Bad actions lead to so-called bad karma. We are the sum of all that we have ever been and done. We are the living embodiment of cosmic cause and effect.

Second, Cayce stressed again and again that "the spirit is life; the mind is the builder; the physical is the result." (349-4) Nothing occurs without the energy of our life-giving spirit. This energy is shaped and focused by the power of our minds, and the material world, including our physical bodies, is the result of this process.

The Origin of Environment and Heredity

Physical is not hereditary!   1310-1

Given these immutable laws and despite appearances to the contrary, cause always flows from the higher, nonphysical realms to the lower, denser, temporal world. Specifically, in studying the readings, I found that the true cause of my inherited illnesses actually originated from a combination of both my past lives and the intervals spent between Earth lives in the dimensions of the planets of our solar system! "[T]he combined influence in an entity's experience . . . becomes . . . the basic influence from heredity and environ; or . . . cause and effect in the experience of an entity." (274-1) In reality, cause and effect created exactly what I merited and exactly what I needed in order to grow. My soul was attracted to the genetics and the circumstances of parents that were suited to the lessons that I needed in this lifetime. When we feel inner urges or emotions rise to the surface, they are literal clues about where we are coming from.

> . . . [that] through which the entity passes become . . . influences . . . in the material plane affecting the entity as Environment or Heredity . . .
>
> The Influences from sojourns in Environs from without the material plane are as . . . *mental* urges that may come as dreams or visions . . . while the Influences from the material sojourns or individual appearances in the Earth are as the earth—earthy *heredity* that may come in . . . the emotions.   1462-1

The astrological sojourns create in our souls subtle urges at the mental level that we can glimpse in our dreams. The hereditary carry-over from our past lives is "earthy" and influences our emotions. Through reincarnation, those whom we have encountered in former lives, we encounter again. These souls then help to create the present environment that we inhabit. It is the time spent in the dimensions of the planets that creates what Cayce calls our spiritual heredity.

> Those that were in the associations, or those that affected the entity during the various experiences through which the entity

> passed . . . are . . . the *entity's* environment, while the sojourns
> become . . . that . . . inherited—or [the] hereditary influence from
> the spiritual viewpoint. 2136-1

Further, physical, mental, and spiritual cause and effect operates differently in the various realms when creating our heredity and environment. Although our past builds our future inheritance and circumstances, we refine and mold what we attract and what we encounter by our use of free will through all of the choices that we make.

> For that which is materially of a hereditary influence is one thing,
> and that which is the hereditary influence of the metaphysical
> and *spiritual* entity is another. Also there is a variation in the
> environmental influences of a material experience and the
> environmentals of the spiritual aspects, according to or because
> of the *abilities* of the mental self . . . to choose! 1580-1

The key variable in shaping our actual situation in any given lifetime is always choice—free will. Our soul decides what the best environmental and hereditary traits are for us to work with at this time. Our own higher self selects which challenges and opportunities we will encounter in this lifetime. Our limitations are instructive, of our own making, and for our own good—always.

Heredity and Karma

Karma is cause oft of hereditary conditions so called. **3313-1**

Cayce began a reading for a young woman in 1941 by saying, "Thus in giving the interpretations of the records here, we would give . . . the . . . hereditary influences; not merely from the material lineage but from the mental and spiritual. For these, too, are a part of the heritage of each and every soul." (2571-1) According to Cayce's source, this causal relationship between physical heredity and the mental and spiritual realms is true for all of us. Our heredity is not only material but mental and spiritual as well.

The following reading is key to understanding Cayce's view of heredity and takes us a step further. It not only states that heredity is really caused by the mind and the choices we have made throughout our eons of experiences, it also ties heredity firmly to karma. For me, this reading was like finding the elusive missing link. It confirmed that my soul knew what I needed in order to grow and had designed and attracted the physical challenges I was experiencing in this lifetime as a learning opportunity. And what a rich and challenging learning experience it has been.

> Thus we find this entity—as each entity—is in the present the result of that the entity has applied of Creative influences and forces in every phase of its experience. Thus it makes for that called by some karma, by others racial hereditary forces.
>
> And thus environment and hereditary forces . . . are in their reality the activities of the *mind* of the entity in its choices through the experiences in the material, in the mental, in the spiritual planes.   1796-1

According to Cayce, karma and heredity are so similar that, from our limited, three-dimensional perspective, they look like the same thing. Thus our present heredity was created by our minds through the use of our wills in making all the past choices that we have made in all of our realms of experience. All of this comes down to something we should be mindful of every day—our choices. How well or how poorly have we applied good in our daily lives? Have we truly tried to do the best we knew to do in our previous experiences, or did we make poor choices that required us to repeat our lessons?

Not only does Cayce tell us straight out that karma is often the cause of our inherited ills, he tells us that what we inherit and will experience is how we have treated our fellow man. This gives a whole new perspective on the golden rule—do unto others as you would have them do unto you. Sooner or later, others will do unto us as we have done unto them, for weal or for woe. And so the cycle continues until we wise up and change our behavior.

Karma is cause oft of hereditary conditions so called. Then

indeed does the soul inherit that it has builded in its experience
with its fellow man in material relationships.   3313-1

The Cayce philosophy led me to understand that my health problems were not only of my own choosing but also in my best long-term
interest. My body is temporary; my soul is eternal. Best of all, both the
present and future health of my body are under my control. I am the
master of my own circumstances.

In summary, our heredity is an effect and not a cause. Our use of free
will in making choices is the real cause. What is the definition of karma
but cause and effect. Thus, as Cayce tells us, heredity and karma are
really the same thing. For all of us, the higher wisdom of our own souls
has programmed in our bodies the design and the exact lessons that we
will need in order to grow in this lifetime. These insights allow us to see
not only purpose but justice in our suffering.

The Effects of Heredity and Environment

. . . the environs and the hereditary influences are spiritual as well
as physical . . .   *852-12*

A common occurrence that frequently puzzles parents is how their
children can be so very different from each other. Cayce provides an
answer to why children born of the same parents and reared in the
same home can look or behave as though they belong to a different
family. He tells us that interplanetary sojourns are often the cause for
the differences between siblings.

. . . for the sojourn in other spheres than earth's plane controls
. . . the *urge* of the individual . . . that would give . . . two
individuals raised under the same environment, of the same
blood . . . different urges.   254-21

For while there . . . is in the experience of every soul the urge that
is termed hereditary and environmental influence, individuals
under the same influence of blood and of rearing (or environment) will respond or react in quite a different manner. This is

caused by that deeper urge that is seen from astrological sojourns, as well as the indwelling in the earth under certain or specific experiences.   816-3

Hence the sojourn of a soul in its environ about the earth, or in this solar system, gives the factors that are often found in individuals in the earth that are of the same parentage, in the same environ; yet one might be a genius and the other a fool; one might be a moral degenerate and the other a high, upright, upstanding individual with an aptitude for influences that may not even be questioned.   541-1

Thus siblings born of and living with their parents can be very different because of having had different planetary consciousness experiences as well as different past lives.

The Role of the Mind in Heredity

. . . the mental body is both finite and infinite, a part of self and yet a part of a universal consciousness— or the mind of the Maker.

1650-1

The readings correlate our heredity with our experiences in planetary dimensions of consciousness and explain that the mechanism is our minds. Mind as a component of our soul is incredibly powerful and works with our spiritual energy, which is our essence and of God. Mind acts as a bridge between the spiritual realms and our physical experiences. It is both physical and nonphysical; it is the bridge between our bodies and our higher selves. Understanding and working constructively with our minds is the key to transforming our karma.

The sojourns in the environs about the earth, or the astrological activities, become a portion then of the influence, such as may be psychologically ascribed to the hereditary influence; or these are inherited influences then and become as innate urges in the experience.   880-2

In a physical reading, Cayce told this seeker that her imagination, which is an aspect of her mind, was exacerbating her health problem:

> These [conditions] have to do with the incoordination of the central nerve and blood supply and the superficial and imaginative system. This does not indicate that the conditions are just imagination, but this does have a great deal to do with the severity—and the physical disturbances become just as great as if these were real in the functioning and organic activity. 3399-1

This same woman was warned again that her tendency toward deafness was mind over matter and that she should take care not to pass on this way of thinking to her children:

> (Q) Is heredity a factor in my loss of hearing?
> (A) Not necessarily, but because others have, you have the consciousness of it—it is a tendency through the suggestive forces.
> (Q) Is it likely to be inherited by offspring?
> (A) If you keep impressing 'em that it may, it may!   3399-1

The following reading explains the difference between this man's hereditary condition and what could be built by his mind. We are thus reminded that the choice and responsibility are always ours. We must guard our thoughts.

> (Q) Is my trouble [the] same as my father had?
> (A) Couldn't be! for the father is one entity and the self is another! It may be of the same *nature*, but it is *not* necessary of a hereditary condition; though thinking it will build just such a condition, of course!   1196-10

Role of the Will in Heredity

. . . ye are not promised more than one day in the physical consciousness at a time. Use it—don't abuse it!   5392-1

Cayce told a young housewife, suffering from a variety of physical ills, that she was subject to the challenges of the body in which her soul had chosen to incarnate. It is helpful to remember that our body's strengths and weaknesses reflect and serve our soul's mental and spiritual purposes.

> So in this body, in this physical condition that exists here with this body, we find it subject to those attributes of a physical being it has chosen for the mental and soul expression of self.   263-13

The greatest single factor in our cosmic journey is always our free will. Edgar told the father of a three–year–old child that the boy's planetary sojourns might not physically influence the child:

> Astrological aspects may or may not become a part of the experience physically for the entity. For these are merely urges, and the will—that which designates God's creation of man from the rest of the animal world—rules as to what an individual soul does with opportunities in relationships with the fellow man.
>   3340-1

Thus, the real determining factor in the relationship between our karma and our heredity is how we have used our wills in making our past choices. These past choices not only create but also limit our present range of options. We are on a self–determined trajectory. Only by engaging our will power can we change our course here on Earth.

> Spiritual heredity, then, is a combination of what the entity or soul has done with its opportunities for creative influence in this and all other experiences. That inherited is what the entity has made of such.   2581-2

Our spiritual heredity flows from all of our past actions. Through all of our past physical and nonphysical experiences, we have had innumerable opportunities to act as a positive and creative influence to other souls. How well we have capitalized on these opportunities puts us right where we are today.

The readings stress over and over again that nothing surpasses our free will. We are truly completely free to choose our own paths. No past life, no astrological sojourn, no karma is more important or influential than our use of will as we try to do the best that we know to do. Our choices become our karma, for weal or woe. At times, the karma we create may seem overwhelming. It is then up to us to reengage our will, shift gears, change our direction, and choose to move forward.

All of these are urges but none of these surpass the will of the entity as a whole—that which is the gift of the Creative Influence or Force, or God, to each soul . . .

Hence in giving the astrological as well as material sojourns, these are relative then according to the application of the will respecting that which the entity sets as its ideal.

That these influences produce then inclinations, or become karmic—as you term—or become an overpowering influence, is only according to the measure of the will in relationship to Creative or God Force in the experience of the entity.   880-2

The Role of the Endocrine Glands in Heredity

. . . the emotions [or] the senses . . . may become a stumbling-stone; as they may for many who tend to satisfy the physical without due mental consideration of spiritual aspects in their experience.   *2021-1*

The readings explain that the endocrine glands are the interface between the physical, mental, and spiritual forces in our bodies. These are the glands that secrete so many powerful hormones into our bloodstream.

. . . there are centers . . . that [are the] contact between the physical, the mental and spiritual.

The spiritual contact is through the glandular forces of creative energies . . .

. . . these become subject not only to the intent and purpose

of the individual entity or soul upon entrance, but are constantly
under the influences of *all* the centers of the mind *and* the
body . . .
    Thus we find the connection, the association of the spiritual
being with the mental self, at those centers from which the
reflexes react to all of the organs, all of the emotions, all of the
activities of a physical body.   263-13

According to Cayce, the importance of these glands cannot be over-
estimated. Their function is controlled by the soul's purpose, and they
are continually influenced by the mind and the body. The glands also
reflex to all of our organs and emotions. According to Cayce, they con-
nect the three parts of our being—spiritual, mental, and physical—in a
very complex fashion that is difficult to grasp:

But there are physical contacts which the anatomist finds not
. . . Yet it is found that within the body there are channels, there
are ducts, there are glands, there are activities that perform no
one knows what! in a living, *moving*, thinking being.   281-41

As if that is not complex enough, Cayce also states:

[. . . the planets] give expression in the abilities, which find
manifestation in the material body through . . . the glandular
system of the body *for* material expression.   2620-2

Furthermore, the readings associate each of the seven spiritual glands
with a planet, and each planet has a unique vibration that is associated
with certain attributes, having both positive and negative aspects. These
traits actually manifest physically through the glands. Remember that
the most influential planet is the one from which our soul took flight to
Earth.

Pituitary—Jupiter (strength, the universal forces)
Pineal—Mercury (mind, mental abilities)
Thyroid—Uranus (extremes, the psychic)

Thymus—Venus (love, beauty, art)
Adrenals—Mars (energy, madness)
Lyden—Neptune (the mystic, attraction to water)
Gonads—Saturn (sudden changes, new starts)

In the Book of Revelation, St. John the Divine addressed the seven churches of Asia, giving their strengths and weaknesses. A unique perspective of the Cayce readings is that these commentaries are symbolic of processes within us and that each church corresponds to an endocrine gland. By studying this material, we can gain additional insights about the role of these powerful and mysterious glands in our own spiritual maturation. The following reading excerpt emphasizes the importance and the power of the endocrine glands for each one of us:

> And it should be considered by all: There is no greater factory in the universe than that in a human body in its natural, normal reacting state. For there are those machines or glands within the body capable of producing, from the very air or water and the food values taken into the body, to take from or to reproduce *any* element *at all* that is *known* in the material world!   1800-21

Good News—What All This Means

. . . no influence of heredity, environment, or what not surpasses the will . . .   5749-14

Here are the major points to keep in mind as we seek to understand the heredity that we carry within us:

1. Our present physical heredity is the result of the choices that we have made in our past lives and in our planetary sojourns.

2. Before we were born, the results of those choices combined to purposefully create karmic effects that manifest as our present heredity and environment—spiritually, mentally, and physically.

3. At a more subtle level, the choices we made during our planetary sojourns manifest as innate mental urges, and our past-life choices manifest through our emotions.

4. The physical–mental–spiritual interface for all of these internal

forces is our endocrine system, comprised of the glands and the nerve plexuses associated with these centers.

5. None of these forces surpass our God–given free will. It's all up to us!

Most importantly, what this all means is that our heredity, like our karma, is not ironclad. It is not irrevocably fixed. We can work to transform hereditary illness by the power of our minds and spirits and, most of all, by our God–given free will.

> (Q) Are hereditary, environment and will equal factors in aiding or retarding the entity's development?
> (A) Will is the greater factor, for it may overcome any or all of the others; provided that will is made one with the pattern, see? For, no influence of heredity, environment or what not, surpasses the will; else why would there have been that pattern shown in which the individual soul, no matter how far astray it may have gone, may enter with Him into the holy of holies?   5749-14

This exciting possibility, that we may transform and heal even our inborn limitations, is really the subject of the rest of this book.

4

We Choose Our Parents!

. . . there is no soul but what the sex life becomes the greater influence in the life . . .   911-2

We choose our parents. This may be good news or bad news, but the Cayce readings assure us that it is true. Each of us chooses our mother and our father and, indirectly, our siblings as our present-life karmic workgroups. Moreover, they also choose us. It's a two-way street, a cooperative agreement, a joint venture, a karmically rich contract of opportunity for all concerned. We're very much all in this together, not only to just get through it but to give it our very best efforts.

Many of us wonder, Why would this be the case? Why would we choose to incarnate with these particular souls with whom we may have vast differences? Again, God's universal laws are always at work. No major relationship is accidental; karma—cause and effect—is always operative. The principle of *like begets like* provides the natural attraction between souls. And we all have free will; it's up to each of us to decide if we're ready to take the plunge and incarnate with these souls whom we've been with before. God's laws provide us the learning opportunities, and I think that all of us would agree that family dynamics are among life's greatest challenges. God is always trying to help us to learn, help us to see what we must do to grow, and is always placing those opportunities right in front of us. We can hardly miss them, even if we don't understand them. We run into them at every turn. And perhaps nowhere is this more true than with the members of our immediate families. Our ties are very long and very deep.

Many of us, especially those who have been abused by a parent, would say, No way! I certainly felt that way. Even after encountering the concept of reincarnation, I was resistant to this idea and denied that I would ever have chosen to incarnate with my father. However, as I pondered this over time, I realized that without this particular father, I would not have had my wonderful grandparents and the very special relationship with my grandfather, who is my twin soul. Upon reflection, I decided that dealing with Dad was definitely worth it, especially if we made some progress. I hope that from his perspective on the other side, he feels the same way toward me.

The River of Life

For, each entity should know that it is not by chance alone, but purposefully and mercifully, that a soul enters.   2539-2

Let's look at how the process of reincarnation within families works. In the language of the readings, how does the infinite manifest in the finite?

> As to appearances in the earth . . . each cycle brings a soul-entity to another crossroad, or another urge from one or several of its activities in the material plane . . . For one enters a material sojourn not by chance, but there is brought into being the continuity of pattern or purpose, and each soul is attracted to those influences that may be visioned from above. Thus *there* the turns in the river of life may be viewed.
>
> To be sure, there are floods in the life; there are dark days and there are days of sunshine. But the soul-entity stayed in a purpose that is creative . . . may find the haven of peace as is declared in Him.   3128-1

This reading offers a great deal of insight into the deeper mechanics of how and why we incarnate when and where we do. Each lifetime brings us to another crossroad from one or more of our previous lives. What must we do at a crossroad? We must choose in which direction we want to go. If we want to move forward, we are forced to make a choice. Our present life is not by chance but is an extension of our own past patterns and purposes. Interestingly, Cayce stresses that our souls are able to view the river of life from on high before we enter our new bodies. We can see how this family constellation will likely flow—in periods of crisis as well as in days full of sunshine. In other words, we know what we're getting into. And here is the key point: If we hold to a creative, constructive purpose, despite the difficulties, we can find a haven of peace. A very hopeful promise indeed.

Although the soul can see beforehand the general family environment it is choosing to enter, these circumstances can sometimes change over time. Regardless, all of these factors will help to strengthen the soul.

> . . . those environs may change; and those activities of individuals may be changed by those influences that appear to be without the scope . . . of man's activity. All of these are oft visioned by the soul before it enters, and all of these are at times met in tempering the soul.   1981-1

Like Begets Like

. . . man . . . finds self as the cause and the product of that [his soul] has gained . . .   *5753-1*

When asking a question about the relation between heredity and the destiny of the body, Edgar's eldest son, Hugh Lynn Cayce, received a very rich response:

> There is a compliance with those things, ever, set as immutable laws. *Like begets like!* Heredity, then, is the association of that within the minds, the bodies, the atomical structural forces of a union which hath drawn for its *own* development as well as for . . . unison of purpose. Hence we have a choice, yet the *choice* of

that as we have built; for as the tree falleth so shall it lie. If the blind lead the blind *both* shall fall into the ditch. But He, the Lord, the Master, the Maker, maketh the paths straight to those, for those, that seek to have *Him* lead the way.   262-82

This reading begins by again emphasizing one of the most important, immutable, unchangeable laws: Like begets like. This is really just another way of explaining karma. What we inherit physically in a new incarnation is a combination of elements from the minds and bodies of our parents. We are also influenced by our parents' purposes and those of our own soul. This is for the benefit of all those involved. The union of these particular parents draws a soul that will further both their own development as well as the development of the incoming soul. The incoming soul has a choice in this matter, which Cayce emphasizes. But here is a very important concept: Cayce's source tells us that our choices now are limited by our former choices. We limit our own present and future range of options by the choices that we have made in previous lives and by what we have built in that process. As an example, Cayce quotes Ecclesiastes 11:3, that where a tree falls, there it lies. This means that in a new incarnation, we must begin where we left off last time. There is continuity in the process. Cayce then interjects some humor from Luke 6:39, which makes another important point by telling us that if the blind lead the blind, they will both fall into a ditch. If, in our new lifetime, we choose blindly, following those who wander through their lives blindly, we will encounter pitfalls. However, if we let God lead us in our choices, we will travel a straight path and avoid falling into ditches.

In a later reading, Hugh Lynn Cayce and the Glad Helpers Prayer Group sought additional information about the formation of the human body:

. . . with the first breath of the infant there comes into being in the flesh a soul — that has been attracted . . . by all the influences and activities that have gone to make up the process through the period of gestation, see?

Many souls are seeking to enter, but not all are attracted. Some may be repelled. Some are attracted and then suddenly repelled, so that the life in the earth is only a few days. Oft the passing of such a soul is accredited to, and *is* because of disease, neglect or the like, but *still* there was the attraction, was there not?

... those mental and physical forces that *are* builded *are* those influences needed *for* that soul that does enter!   281-53

Here we are shown some of the dynamics behind a soul's decision to reincarnate, if only for a short time. An infant attracted to a new body becomes a soul in the flesh when it draws its first breath. Recognizing the growth opportunities implicit in reincarnating, many souls want to enter the earth plane but may or may not be attracted to a particular family. Some souls may even be repelled by a given incarnation opportunity. When a soul incarnates and then is suddenly repelled, perhaps by a change in circumstance, the soul withdraws and the child dies.

Although the outer cause may appear to be disease or neglect, Cayce tells us that there is a deeper cause. Despite the soul's ability to view the family's river of life and its probable path from the other side, it was attracted and chose to incarnate briefly. Tragically, the soul's withdrawal would be extremely painful for the child's family, especially if they did not have a higher, spiritual perspective.

The Parents' Purposes

Hence those who consider the manner of being channels through which souls may enter are taking hold upon God-Force itself ...

281-55

The readings frequently state that the purpose in which we act is of paramount importance, and this is especially true when using our God-given life force to create a new channel for a soul to incarnate. Cayce calls this "the *opportunity* of conception." (281-46)

Man was given the ability to create through self a channel through which ... spirit might ... manifest in a material world ... [T]here needs be first that of desire, purpose. It is known as a fact that this may be wholly of the carnal or animal nature on the part

of even one, and yet conception may take place; and the end of
that physical activity is written in that purpose and desire . . .

The ideal manner . . . is that there may be a channel through
which the spirit of truth, hope, divine knowledge and purpose,
may be made manifest . . .

Desire . . . creates certain forces about which there is a physical
nucleus that is the pattern of the universe . . . that form that
vibration upon which that individual entity *will* or *does* vibrate
at its . . . conception . . .

Thus the greater unison of purpose, of desire, at a period of
conception brings the more universal consciousness—or being—for a perfect or equalized vibration for that conception.

281-46

Let's examine some of the powerful concepts set forth in this reading.
The central point of the whole reading is powerfully stated: "[T]he end
of that physical activity is written in that purpose and desire!" The purpose of a sexual union that results in a new vehicle for a soul is the
ultimate creative act and has a profound impact on which souls are
attracted. Conception that is only carnal in purpose will attract a soul of
similar vibration and purpose.

Ideally, the parents will so conduct themselves that they will attract a
soul with divine knowledge and purpose. The partners' desire, which is
an aspect of mind (and mind is always the builder), creates an actual
physical nucleus at a particular rate of vibration that attracts a soul of
that vibration. The more the desires of both parents are in accord during conception, the more the vibration is equalized, or perfected, to
attract an appropriate soul.

The Incoming Soul's Purposes

. . . the hope of the world rests upon the developing *minds, the*
younger *generations . . .*   *4113-1*

From the point of view of the incoming soul, there may be various
purposes for incarnating. Cayce told a forty-seven-year-old widow that
she had a strong purpose for entering:

> As each soul enters in the earth, there are purposes other
> than that which may be arising from desire of those that
> physically are responsible for such an advent.
>
> For, the soul seeks from the realm of spirituality to give
> expression of that it as an entity or soul may do with its experi-
> ences in the mental realm, as well as about that it *has* done in a
> physical realm.

Her reading begins by explaining that a soul's purpose in entering is
far more than just the result of the physical desire of the parents. The
incoming soul seeks an opportunity to express the results of what it has
done and what it has learned during its time in the nonphysical planetary realms as well as in its past lives.

> Hence the law that is ever present; like attracts like; like begets
> like. Hence there is the attraction as from the desires of those in
> the physical calling to the sources of generation in the flesh, to
> the sources of creation or of spirit in the spiritual realm.

The Source reminded her that the universal laws of God always rule.
Like attracts and always begets like. The parents and the incoming soul
are attracted to each other. The Source explains poetically that this attraction results from the desires of the parents in the flesh calling to
those souls in the spiritual realm, who then become the next generation
in the flesh.

> Hence there is often a real purpose in the soul, as in this soul,
> seeking a period of expression of self; and finding it in that about
> the bodies when there is the period of presentation. For, while
> the physical begins at conception, the spiritual and mental is as
> the first breath taken into the physical—that becomes then a
> living soul, with a physical organism for manifestation during the
> sojourn in that particular experience.

Here Cayce tells this woman that she, like many souls, has a particular purpose. She seeks to express herself and finds the opportunity in

this particular conception. Interestingly, the reading clarifies that physical life begins at conception but that it becomes a living soul when the spirit and mind enter as the first breath is taken.

> Then, what influences such a journey, such an advent of the soul from the unseen into materiality? Development of the soul that it may take its place, through the lessons gained in physical experience, in those classes or realms of soul activity in an infinite world—among those that have passed in their activity through the various realms; seeking then (as that which first called every soul and body into experience) that of companionship.   541-1

The Source then returns to the basic purpose for reincarnation and asks rhetorically, Why, then, does a soul enter materiality? It is that the soul may continue to develop as a result of all of its past lessons on Earth and elsewhere. And, as always, the ultimate purpose for soul growth is to be a fit companion to our Creator.

According to the Cayce readings, the potential of conception is far, far greater than we realize. Not only our souls, but our minds and even our bodies, are virtually unlimited:

> For, within the nucleus at conception is the pattern of all that is possible. And remember, man—the soul of man, the body of man, the mind of man—is nearer to limitlessness than anything in creation.   281-55

However, with the gift of almost limitless potential comes great responsibility: "To whom much has been given, of them much is expected, much is required." (1981-1) The beautiful biblical example that follows demonstrates how parents can realize this divine potential.

Abraham and Sarah—A Cayce Study

(Q) Conception can only take place when the spiritual ideal set by both [parents] is met.
(A) True *conception,* spiritual *conception,* mental *conception only*

takes place under such . . .   *281-55*

In the next reading, Cayce uses a famous example taken from the Old Testament to describe how the process of spiritual conception can actually work:

> When Abraham and Sarah were given the promise of an heir through which the nations of the earth would be blessed, there were many years of preparation of these individuals, of the physical, mental and spiritual natures . . .
>
> Here we find, then, that mind and matter are coordinated into bringing a channel for spiritual activity that is not exceeded in any of the characters depicted in Holy Writ.
>
> . . . there was a perfect coordination in and through the whole period of gestation . . .
>
> . . . also . . . throughout the period of gestation the activities about . . . the mother, were such as to *influence* the entity yet unborn, in patience to a degree not manifested in any other of the patriarchs. While the physical conditions made manifest in the body during the growth into manhood were affected by *material* laws, there was not the changing or deviating whatsoever from the spiritual through the mental.
>
> Hence we have that illustration of what may be termed the individual ideally conceived, ideally cherished and nourished through the periods of gestation.   281-48

Cayce tells us that Abraham and Sarah underwent many years of physical, mental, and spiritual preparation. It was not an overnight occurrence. The coordination of the mental and physical aspects throughout the entire pregnancy was so perfect that the channel for the incoming soul (Isaac) was the most perfect for spiritual activity of any character in the Bible.

In addition, we are told that Sarah's patience during her pregnancy exceeded any of the patriarchs in the Old Testament and greatly influenced her unborn child. Moreover, throughout Isaac's youth, she held firmly to the spirit of the promise that she and Abraham had been given. This is what can occur when a child is ideally conceived, cherished, and nourished. A special soul may enter and bless many.

For the Benefit of All

Ye grow in grace, in knowledge, in understanding.   **1436-1**

As both the Bible and the readings tell us, God's law is perfect. Although the world appears to be anything but perfect, the process of soul attraction and reincarnation benefits all those involved. Cause and effect—karma—is really a win–win situation. We enter the very situation that we need to in order to grow with those who will help us, even as we will help them. God designed it that way, but our own choices determine the level of difficulty and our degree of success.

> For what purpose then entered ye into this experience? That thy earthly father, that thy earthly mother brought by a union a consummation of a material desire the opportunity for thy soul to seek expression again in materiality—for it offered thee the opportunities for thy aid to each of them, their aid, their counsel, their guidance to thee that ye might be the better channel.
>
> For as ye viewed from the ramparts of that inter-between thy activities in the material world, ye found a means of expression of that *thou art*—*in* the mercy of the Lord!   **1440-2**

Even though our new body may have been the result of our parents' physical desires, it not only provided a new vehicle for our souls but an opportunity for us to help them as well. Conversely, as all parents know, it also afforded them many years of opportunities to care for and guide us as we grew. We are reminded that we knew what we were getting into; we could see this family's river of life from on high. It was a mutually beneficial situation, provided by the mercy of our Creator, in which we could express all that we are.

Although the growth potential of the circumstances in the new family may be just what is needed for all concerned when viewed from the higher, spiritual perspective, life is anything but easy. At times it can be very, very hard, especially for those who look only at their physical existence and ignore higher spiritual reality. Cayce counseled many people in crises and heartbreak who came to him in desperation. The parents of this two-year-old child suffering with cancer were told that their son's situation was very bleak:

> As we find, conditions are very serious. There should not be too great a stress put upon determining to hold this body in material manifestations. Not that the hope and trust in the divine is to be lessened. Rather should it be exercised the more in realizing . . . what the handicaps would be. These should give rather the parents, those so close, the feeling of their interest, of their witness before the throne of grace and mercy.
>
> There are physical disturbances that are a part of the entity's karma. They are for lessons for those responsible for the body, if ye will accept it. If ye let it harden thee, ye miss the opportunity of knowing that He is the resurrection, He is the truth and life.
>
> Put thy child rather at all times into the arms of Jesus.
>
> In the physical we would apply those conditions that may aid. As developments progress, let that which is of the divine deter-mine whether it is best in this consciousness or in the universal consciousness that it is to serve.   3391-1

It is very difficult to perceive the tragedy of a terminally ill child as grace and mercy. But if we try to look deeper, with spiritual eyes, we can see that there is much more that may be understood. The parents were told that the child was so very seriously ill that it would be best not to try to hold him in his physical body. This would only imprison him in a diseased body, prolong his suffering, and cause much sorrow for all. It helps to remember that the child's soul knew what to expect and chose to incarnate into these circumstances. If the intended lessons are learned, not endeavoring to unnaturally lengthen the child's painful experience may then be seen as a form of grace and mercy for all the family.

The reading goes on to say that although the physical problems are part of the child's karma, the situation is a lesson for the parents if only they can see and accept it. If the parents allow their grief to blind them to the larger truths and cause them to become embittered, they will miss the opportunity of understanding that ultimately, it is the spirit and not the physical that is life. It is best if they can bow to the higher plan, of which their souls are aware, and turn over their love and pain for their child to Him whom Cayce called the "pattern" for life in the Earth.

Cayce went on to give physical suggestions to help relieve the child's suffering, and he urged the parents to let the divine decide if it were better for the child's soul to continue to serve in the physical plane or in the nonphysical universal consciousness.

Six weeks after this reading was given, a close friend of the child's family sent the following letter to Edgar Cayce:

> I just wanted to thank you again for the reading of little [3391].
> He died about three weeks ago, but he died quietly and peace-
> fully, without pain. His mother followed the directions carefully
> and the reading helped her to bear his passing. We are very
> grateful for your help.   3391-1, R1

It seems from this letter that the child's parents took the higher road. Despite their anguish, they not only faithfully followed Cayce's physical suggestions to alleviate the child's suffering but also gained a measure of peace from the reading's spiritual counsel. I think that we may assume that this little boy's short life span brought healing and spiritual growth to all of them.

Both the Bible and the readings tell us many times that no matter how difficult the challenge we face, God always allows us a way to meet it in a constructive manner. No matter how blocked we feel in a situation, we can make choices that are in keeping with our soul's purpose if we choose to do so. We can "enlarge" our soul and move closer to the purpose for which we were created. Through the way of spirit, we find the answers we need:

> For, remember, He hath not willed that any soul should perish,
> but hath with each temptation, with each experience offered
> . . . a choice whereby the soul is enlarged, is shown that the choice
> brings it nearer . . . to that purpose for which expression is given
> . . . in the material world; even as He, the way, the life, the truth,

came into life in materiality that we, through Him might have the advocate with the Father, and thus in Him find the answer to every problem in material experience.   1981-1

The Cayce readings say that the statement that God has not willed that any soul should perish (II Peter 3:9) is the truest statement in the Bible. We are always given a choice, a way out of our temptations. One of these opportunities is that our Creator "has allowed each . . . to be born as a babe, and to thus have a new opportunity. This has made that act of motherhood, that act of babes being born into the earth, as a special indication of God's love." (1152-9)

Part II:
Karma–Cosmic Cause and Effect

... the earth is a causation world, for in the earth, cause and effect are as the natural law. And as each soul enters this material plane, it is to meet or to give those lessons or truths that others, too, may gain the more knowledge of the purpose for which each soul enters.

3645-1

Thus each experience, as will be indicated in the sojourns through a material plane, is meeting self. For, as has been given of old, "That which I hated has come upon me." The slights, the slurs ye speak of others will be as thy chickens come home to roost.

2154-1

5

Karma–Unfinished Business

Each soul pays for his own shortcomings, not someone else's!
1056-2

Now that we've explored how the law of reincarnation works, we'll study its corollary—the law of karma. The Cayce readings contain many fascinating and moving examples of bewildered and suffering souls who came seeking an understanding of their challenges and pain. Of course, few people came to him asking why they enjoyed so many blessings in their lives, which are also karmic. The readings are rich in their discussion of what karma is and how it works. Most importantly, Cayce's source eloquently explains the purpose and benevolence of this exacting universal law.

What Is Karma?

For, His laws will not be mocked, and what any individual sows,
that it eventually reaps. 2079-1

What is karma? How does it work? Is everything that happens to us caused by karma? How can we change or heal our karma? These are some of the common questions that people ask. We can best answer these questions by consulting the wisdom that flowed through Edgar Cayce.

The *Random House Unabridged Dictionary* defines karma as action which brings upon oneself inevitable results, good or bad, either in this life or in a reincarnation.[1] This ancient concept is a central belief in both Hinduism and Buddhism. One of Cayce's greatest contributions to Western thinking is his integration of these very important but traditionally Eastern concepts into Christianity.

The readings define karma in several different ways:

> Karmic conditions, of course, are cause and effect.   3249-1

> For it is a universal and divine law that like begets like.
>   1472-13

> *Karma* is . . . the lack of living to that *known* to do!   2271-1

> Thus each experience . . . is meeting self.   2154-1

> What is karma but giving way to impulse?   622-6

Cayce's readings tell us how karma began:

> In the beginning all souls were as a unity to the God-Force. As self added or subtracted that which was in keeping with God's purpose, ye added or subtracted from the blessings ye might be conscious of in materiality. Thus karma is builded. And the law is perfect—what ye sow, ye reap.
>
> There is no law causing man to separate himself from his Maker. There is no cause except man's own indulgence or neglect.   3660-1

When we were created as souls, we were one with God. As we used our free will in different ways, we built karma for ourselves. If we used it in harmony with God's will, we built good karma. If we used our will selfishly, we built bad karma and separated from our Creator, which made our lives harder. God's laws are perfect. We must reap what we have sown.

I think of karma as cosmic cause and effect. The idea of some cause having an effect sounds pretty simple in theory. But, as we all know, meeting and dealing with our life issues can feel overwhelming. This is especially true if we don't understand what is really happening and don't have the spiritual insights and tools to work creatively with our challenges.

We don't just want to meet our karma; we want to resolve it, heal it, and transform it into grace so that our struggles serve the intended purpose and we grow. Buddha is credited with this beautiful definition of karma: "The heart of it is Love, the end of it is Peace and consumma-tion sweet."[2] This captures the motivation, essence, and spirit of karmic law, which is always love. These laws are immutable:

> Know that there are unchangeable laws which find their incep-tion . . . in the spirit of things, of times, of conditions, of individuals who also act with and towards such; and these find a material expression in, namely: As ye sow, so shall ye reap; with what manner of measure ye mete unto others it shall be meted unto thee; if ye would create confidence in thyself, *find and have* confidence in others; see in thy fellow man, though he may be thy enemy, that *motivating* force or power or spirit ye would worship in thy Maker! 2419-1

A classic Cayce definition of karma is meeting oneself and all that self has created. We human beings are very complex creatures; we lead very complex lives. Look at all that we have done in just this one lifetime. Consider all of our relationships, all of our interactions, and all of the places we've been. Worse yet—consider all of our thoughts! Yes, we an-swer for our thoughts too. The readings stress that thoughts are things and are just as real. The Bible tells us that what we lust after in our hearts and minds is just as real as if we actually acted on those desires. (Matthew 5:28)

It is crucial to remember that karma is a neutral and unchangeable law. It is not punishment, nor is it random. We are not victims. It would make no sense to just reincarnate over and over again without there being a corrective mechanism to educate us and show us how we are doing. It is through meeting our karma that we can learn and decide to alter our behavior, thereby advancing. Our conscious minds do not re-member our past-life experiences, because the conscious mind, like the physical body, did not reincarnate. But our subconscious minds remain a part of us and remember everything. Karma is simply cause and effect neutrally manifesting in some form or circumstance. Remember that God is no respecter of persons. As it says in the Bible, "He makes his sun to rise on the evil and on the good, and sends rain on the just and on the unjust." (Matthew 5:45)

This twenty-nine-year-old man was worried about working out his karma. The Source explained the larger issues at hand.

> (Q) Have I much bad karma to work out in this life?
> (A) *Karma* is rarely understood, in "being *worked out*." There is, has been prepared, a way in which karma—as ordinarily known—may be forgiven thee. There are constantly those necessary temptations being presented before each soul, each individual, ... that [if] left [to the Godly] Forces ... rather than to self, there is *little* to be feared in that that would beset.   311-7

God's laws are benevolent. We constantly encounter temptations, which are necessary opportunities to heal and forgive the past tres-passes that created our present challenges. If we trust in this higher process and do our best, there is little to worry about. In reality, there is no such thing as good or bad karma. Although these terms are com-monly used, it is just a convenience for discussion purposes. Karma is a natural, neutral law designed to teach us back to our divine state of consciousness. Thus, all karma is good karma, even if it is temporarily painful, because we will learn from it.

> Remember, the things you applied once—now you are meeting them! Live with this in mind (and every soul may take heed): *Ye shall pay every whit, that ye break of the law of the Lord.* For the

> law of the Lord is perfect; it converteth the soul.   3359-1

Here lies the key to understanding the law of karma. It is educational; it teaches us; it converts our souls. Our Earth is a very sticky and "karmalized" plane of existence, and karma can be very hard to digest. Karma is self-inflicted. We limit ourselves through our past choices. Those choices create and attract the circumstances and people we later encounter. Our free will really determines our fate. How we choose to meet our karma literally creates our future.

The next reading clarifies how we carry our karma within us. Karma does not exist between people; it exists between us and ourselves.

> (Q) Is there some karmic debt to be worked out with either or both [parents] and should I stay with them until I have made them feel more kindly toward me?
> (A) These—What *is* karmic debt? This ye have made a bugaboo! . . .
>
> And whether it be . . . activities to those who have individualized as thy father, thy mother, thy brother . . . or others, it is merely self being *met*, in relationships to that they *themselves* are working out and not a karmic debt *between* but a karmic debt of *self* that may be worked out *between* the associations that exist in the present! And this is true for every soul.   1436-3

Cayce's source stresses over and over again that karma is meeting self, not someone else. Our present relationships and circumstances, which are manifested by our choice to incarnate, give all involved the opportunity to meet what each of us has built within ourselves.

We build karma in the little everyday things in life that are the coin of our daily thoughts and reactions. It is through all that we do each and every day that we demonstrate our level of spiritual consciousness:

> For, as ye live, as ye make manifestations, ye show in thy daily life who is thy Master, who walketh with thee. Do ye show forth sorrow, do ye show forth grudges, do ye show forth little petty hatreds? These are not—as ye know—of the spirit of truth; they

are those things that bring sorrow, sadness, disappointments, shadows of the evil things.   1404-1

For know, this is another law: To know and to misuse is sin. To have knowledge and misapply it is man's undoing.   1152-4

What Is Not Karma?

Yet, karmic is that brought over, while cause and effect may exist in the one material experience only.   *2981-2*

Cayce makes a distinction between karma and short-term cause and effect. Strictly speaking, karma is cause and effect that is carried over from a previous lifetime. But we all recognize that cause and effect can also occur more quickly and manifest in the same lifetime. For example, if a student doesn't study for an exam, he or she will not do well. If we don't take care of our bodies, they will develop health problems, and so forth. In everyday instances like these, it is usually easy to see this cause-and-effect relationship. It's our unconscious, past-life karma that we often have difficulty understanding.

From this point of view, it may seem like everything in life is karmic, but the readings indicate that this is not the case. Although we live in a cause-and-effect universe, Cayce allows that even though there are no coincidences in life, there are accidents.

(Q) Was there a spiritual cause for the accident to my right hand, or was it purely an accident? Is it possible to rectify it?
(A) It was purely an accident; not a spiritual cause. If ye give it power over thee, it may not be rectified—that is, by holding to any thought of payment.   3051-2

In this reading, Cayce went on to give this forty-five-year-old house-wife a remedy that he said would strengthen her injured hand considerably. However, she was warned that if she allowed her mind to dwell on this incident and hold a grudge, her injury, which was accidental, might not be fully healed.

A fifty-two-year-old woman asked Cayce what karmic debts she was paying in this lifetime to have had eight surgeries. He clarified the role of karmic carry-over versus simple cause and effect in her present life by telling her that she had not taken good care of her body:

> It is not the paying for karmic debts of other experiences so much as the lack of conformity to the laws as pertaining to health in the various environs in which the body has found itself, or labored, in this experience.   2067-3

Another example of something not being karmic is the work of those souls who volunteer for difficult tasks and incarnate to serve others. The classic example in the Bible is the man who was born blind (see John 9:1-3). Here Jesus said that in this case, the purpose of the man's blindness was to allow God's healing power to work through him.

> Let that be considered as was given by Him, who is Life and the Light and the Way—to His disciples concerning the man born blind. "Who sinned, this man or his parents that he was born blind?" Let the answer as He gave be thy strength, yea thy knowledge in Him, "Neither this man *nor* his parents but that the love of the Father might be *now* made manifest among the children of men."   1504-1

Like reincarnation, the concept of one who voluntarily returns from the heavens to help others is found in Buddhism. Such a person is called a Bodhisattva. The dictionary defines a Bodhisattva as one who has attained enlightenment but who postpones entering nirvana in order to help others attain enlightenment.[3] This concept is also found in the Cayce readings and is discussed in chapter 15.

There is another occurrence in life that may not be karmic. As we saw in chapter 2, Cayce called our flesh experience in this Earth school "the testing portion of the universal vibration." We incarnate in circumstances that are conducive to encountering necessary tests in a way that is helpful to us. The biblical Book of Job tells the story of the painful testing that a man named Job endured. In the first chapter, God calls Job "a blameless and upright man." Satan then challenges God and says that

God has richly blessed Job, but should these blessings be taken away, Job will "curse You to Your face." God allows Satan to test everything in Job's life but not to kill him. Job unhappily endures great suffering, and a friend chides him, "[H]appy is the man whom God corrects; therefore do not despise the chastening of the Almighty." After a long journey of painful self-examination, Job acknowledges God's justice, humbles himself, and submits. God then blesses Job even more richly than before, and he goes on to live another 140 years. (Job 1–42)

As an interesting note, the Cayce readings say that the Book of Job was written by Melchizedek, an ancient and mysterious biblical figure. The readings further state that Melchizedek was an early incarnation of the Master Soul, whom we later know as Jesus. (262-55) Therefore, given this, it seems likely that Job's story was written as an allegory to instruct all mankind. Thus, we may encounter earthly afflictions that are not karmic in order to see if we have truly learned our lessons.

When a thirty–three–year–old engineer asked Cayce if the loss of his leg in an accident was due to a karmic debt, Cayce replied that this was not the case: "This is an experience that is necessary for thy better unfoldment. Not as in payment for something, but that ye might know the truth that might set you free." (2981-1) Apparently, this soul recognized that attaining spiritual truth and freedom would be best served by experiencing the loss of a limb, and he made the very tough decision to meet that experience.

Thus, considering the world about us, it is good to keep in mind that all the ills that we see are not necessarily the hand of karma. Some of those who suffer physical or mental challenges or who are struck by disaster may have chosen their experiences for their own soul growth or to assist in the growth of those about them. We certainly should not assume that someone who is poor, ill, or handicapped is guilty of some past transgression. He or she may be serving a high spiritual purpose that is hidden from view.

In the final analysis, it really doesn't matter whether the cause of our problems is karmic or not. If we seek to meet all our challenges to the best of our ability, we are accomplishing our true mission. A case in point is a thirty–four–year–old woman who requested a series of readings from Cayce, seeking help regarding a stomach that was too small.

When she asked what the karmic cause was, he told her not to focus on the karma but to do her spiritual work: "Let's leave karma out. For there is a way, and the trust is in the divine within that may be in attune[ment] with the infinite. The karma—well, these would be sad. Leave this out. Just change it." (2072-14)

The readings assure us that opportunities to grow are always before us. "For no contact, no acquaintance, no friend, no—not even a foe or a passing acquaintance is without purpose in same." (1404-1)

How Does Karma Work?

For if there is trouble in thy mind, in thy body, in thy spirit—or pur- pose . . . sin lieth at that door. **1537-1**

Both the Old and New Testaments support the concept found in the Cayce readings that karma is caused by sin:

. . . if you do not do well, sin lies at the door. Genesis 4:7

Sin no more, lest a worse thing come upon you. John 5:14

God is speaking to Cain in the first quote, from Genesis. Jesus is speaking to the man He healed by the pool of Bethesda in the second quote. Cayce is in the best possible company when he warns us that our troubles, physically, mentally, and spiritually, are the results of sin. We all have troubles, and being told by such august sources that their cause is sin is very sobering. *Sin* is a very loaded word in our culture. But Cayce has a wonderfully pithy definition of sin: "For selfishness is sin." (254-87) We need to face the truth that we have all erred in selfishness. When we place our own interests and desires above others, we are sin- ning and trouble will follow.

In a reading requested by the A.R.E. prayer group, Cayce stated that when Jesus healed the man who was sick with palsy, He was publically recognizing that sin had caused the man's illness (Matthew 9: 2-6):

. . . when He said to him sick of the palsy, "Son, thy sins be forgiven thee." When the questionings came (as He knew they

would), He answered "Which is it easier to say, Thy sins be
forgiven thee, or Arise, take up thy bed and go unto thine house?"
. . . For, the question was not as to whether He healed but as to
whether He had the power to forgive sin! The recognition was
that sin had caused the physical disturbance.   5749-16

Cayce also offers another perspective on sin. He tells us that there "is
another law: To know and to misuse is sin. To have knowledge and
misapply it is man's undoing." (1152-4) When we knowingly do not do
what we know we should do, we are sinning by putting ourselves and
our desires first. Actually, Cayce's definition of sin as selfishness is very
close to his definition of karma as meeting self. The reason is quite
simple. All too frequently, we misuse our free will when we consciously
choose to indulge in the gratification of our lower self's desires rather
than take the high road.

We cannot escape what we have created. Our karma continues to
travel with us until we meet it successfully at the level at which we
originally created it. "What you sow in the flesh you reap in the flesh.
What you sow in the spirit, in the mind, you reap in the mind." (1387-1)
Bemoaning our difficulties or wallowing in self-pity is a pointless waste
of time. We are today right where we need to be:

> For, know, each soul merits that condition, that position it *today*
> occupies! But be not *thou* the judge. Rather *open* the way that
> new hope, new light, new joy, new aspirations may be in the
> hearts and minds of those ye would serve.   262-121

> As we as individuals apply the self in a given direction there is a
> growth, there is a greater understanding; thus opening for self
> other experiences that must be met. For did He not give,
> "Heavens and the earth may pass, but my law, my word, shall
> remain?" And each soul must pay every whit—in what? In the
> knowledge, in the understanding that as ye mete it must be meted
> to you.   1189-1

It is comforting to remember that it is God's purpose and desire that

we grow to become His worthy companions. Remembering the following beautiful words from Cayce can provide strength and encouragement:

> For this experience is for thy own holiness, if ye will but look to
> Him. For God hath not willed that any soul should be in shame,
> in discouragement, bound with the fetters of circumstance or of
> obligation, but would have thee *free*—as He hath given thee
> thine *own* will—yea, thine own soul, and said, "If ye will be my
> son, I will be thy God."
>
> Hast thou drawn away? Hast thou neglected thy sonship, thy
> kinship with thy Maker?
>
> Have ye looked upon the circumstances of others and envied
> them, or coveted their position or their place? Then, know ye
> have brought condemnation to thine own self!
>
> Face the light of truth, as is set in Him, and the shadows of
> doubt and fear, of disappointments and sorrow, will fall far, far
> behind! For ye will enter into that peace as He hath promised, "If
> ye will ask, if ye will live in me, I will come and abide with thee."
>
> 1759-1

In 1932 two good questions about karma were asked by members of
the healing group formed as part of Cayce's work.

> (Q) When one is working out a karma, is it right to try to help that
> one?
> (A) . . . When there are karmic conditions in the experience of an
> individual, that [which] designates those that have the Christ-
> like spirit is not only in praying for them, holding meditation for
> them, but aiding, helping, in every manner that the works of God
> may be manifest in their lives, and *every* meditation or prayer:
> *Thy will, O God, be done in that body as Thou seest best. Would*
> *that this cup might pass from me, not my will but Thine be done!*
>
> (Q) How do we know when to help an individual?
> (A) Do with thy might what thine hands, hearts, minds, souls,
> find to do, leaving the increase, the benefits, in *His* hands, who

is the Giver of all good and perfect gifts. Be not faint hearted because, as thou seest, that is not accomplished in the moment. What is eternity to a single experience? "No good thought shall return to me empty handed." Believest thou? Then thou knowest, then, that that as is given out *must* return full measure.   281-4

Cayce spells it out clearly. We should always help other people. It doesn't matter that a problem may be karmic. We should pray and meditate and help others in every way that we can while holding the highest of intentions—that God's will may be done.

Cayce's response to the second question is really a lesson in how karma works. Do your best and leave the rest to God. Have faith and focus on the long-term—eternity. Know that what you give out returns to you in kind. If it seems at times that someone's karmic burden is overwhelming, be assured that this is not the case. Karma is an invitation to serious work. (In the next four chapters, we'll look at many examples as well as some particular types of karma.)

Meeting Our Karma

Remember, ye cannot run away from thyself.   *1776-1*

Let's look at some of Cayce's approaches to meeting our karma. Since one definition of karma is not doing the best that we know to do, forgiveness of ourselves and others is a very good place to start.

Karma is rather the lack of living to that *known* to do! As ye would be forgiven, so forgive in others. *That* is the manner to meet karma.   2271-1

Remember that basically, karma is cause and effect. What we think, say, or do comes back to us sooner or later. Therefore, self-evaluation is another very helpful suggestion from Cayce.

Thus as we find in the experiences in the earth, one only meets self. Learn, then, to stand oft aside and watch self pass by—even in those influences that at times are torments to thy mind.   3292-1

The readings stress that in life, we meet ourselves over and over again—ourselves, not someone else. How well do we really know ourselves? Do we ever take a good, hard look at ourselves? How objective can we be about ourselves and our actions toward others? Have we ever really tried to honestly and objectively analyze our problems and examine our own role in creating them? Or do we find it more comfortable to blame someone else—perhaps our parents, our spouse, our boss, or even God?

Let's take a common issue—ill will between people. Unfortunately, there's plenty of that to go around in our world. All of us have had the experience of speaking in haste and wishing we could take back our words. All of us have been critical or judgmental of others. All of us have uneven relationships with other people, some better than others. Select one of your less comfortable relationships, someone who you avoid if you can. Try to step back and objectively examine your own role and shortcomings in the relationship. In the spirit of working with our karma through both self-evaluation and forgiveness, consider this rhetorical question from Cayce: "For if ye would not forgive, how may ye expect to be forgiven?" (633-5) If we want someone to forgive something we have said or done, we can create some good karma by being willing to forgive them first. Recognizing one's own role in a sour relationship can make it easier to take the first step and reach out. Regardless of the apparent outcome, the sincerity of this effort within one's own heart and mind will yield some positive karma sometime, in some way. We need to trust the process and continue without seeking external verification. Just do your best and leave it to the Lord.

> **Even as He, the Master gave, the faults ye find in others are reflected in thine own mirror of life. And as He gave, "Cast the beam out of thine eye that ye may see to take the mote from thy brother's eye."** 3395-2

It's a very sobering thought that the faults we see in others are also in us. We need to start with ourselves and take an inner inventory. This effort can be very challenging and illuminating, to say the least. It's an ongoing, lifelong process, not a one-time thing. Try it periodically. Be sure to make some notes, and date them for future comparison. You'll be able to see how far you've come. These insights are deeply personal and very valuable if we are really serious about spiritual growth.

A young student asked Cayce the following question:

> (Q) How can I make good karma from this period?
> (A) . . . Lose self in the consciousness of the *indwelling* of the Creative Force, in that channel as has been prepared for the escape of the sons *and* daughters of men, through the *Son* of man! This is the escape, and what to be done about it! Lose self; make His will one with *thy* will, or thy will be lost in *His* will, being a *channel* through which He may manifest in the associations of self with the sons and daughters of men!   275-23

In this guidance to a seventy-year-old woman, Cayce gave universal advice about how to meet one's karma:

> If the experiences are ever used for self-indulgence, self-aggrandizement, self-exaltation, each entity does so to its *own* undoing, or creates for self that as has been termed or called karma—and must be met. And in meeting every error, in meeting every trial, in meeting every temptation—whether these be mental or really physical experiences—the manner and purpose and approach to same should be ever in that attitude, "Not my will but Thine, O God, be done in and through me."   1224-1

In summary, the readings are very clear about the best way to meet our karma. Cayce told this man, who was very ill, what he needed to do.

> Thus we find what is commonly called the law of cause and effect, or karmic conditions being met by an individual entity. For, as given of old, each soul shall give an account of every idle word spoken. . .
>   The entity, then, is still at war with itself, but all hate, all malice, all that would make man afraid, must be eliminated, first from the mind of the individual entity . . .

Then, right about *face!* *Know* that the Lord liveth, and would
do thee good—if ye will but trust wholly in Him!   3124-1

Some additional, specific ideas from the readings about meeting and
healing karma and moving into grace will be shared in Part III.

6

Our Karmic Bodies

For resentments of any nature bring their fruit in the physical.

288-37

Types of Physical Karma

Keep the physical fit that the soul may manifest the longer. 294-7

In her classic work on Edgar Cayce's story of reincarnation and karma, *Many Mansions*, Dr. Gina Cerminara divided physical karma into three categories: boomerang, organismic, and symbolic. As the name indicates, boomerang karma is an action toward another person that rebounds to the originator of the action. Organismic karma occurs when someone misuses a bodily organ in one life and inherits difficulty with the same organ in another life. Symbolic karma is more subtle and is seen when a past–life wrong yields a more general, chronic, and illusive bodily challenge in a later life.[1] As we explore examples of physical karma from the Cayce readings, we will see some examples of these three different types.

Cayce's Karmic Conditions

... all illness is sin; not necessarily of the moment, as man counts
time, but as a part of the whole experience.   3395-2

Edgar Cayce is perhaps most famous as the "father of holistic medicine." In addition to the physical relief Cayce's readings brought to so
many suffering souls, the readings' insightful spiritual and mental counsel, together with their past-life and interplanetary information, wove a
complete and unique tapestry of the true cause of illness. As we look at
some specific examples of physical karma from the readings, we can see
some of these threads.

Acne, allergies, anemia, asthma, bed-wetting, blindness, bronchitis,
cancer, deafness, eczema, epilepsy, foot problems, gonorrhea, hyperten-
sion, insanity, melancholia, multiple sclerosis, muscular dystrophy,
obesity, paralysis, Parkinson's disease, polio, and possession—the Cayce
readings describe the influence of karma in an amazing array of diseases and health concerns. However, we must keep in mind that these
readings were given for specific individuals and that each of us is
unique. Although we can't always generalize from these cases, some of
the approaches may be helpful in healing our own ills:

A forty-year-old woman suffering with allergies was told that she
had been a chemist in a prior life who used many things to produce
itching in others. Cayce said, "She finds it in herself in the present!"
(3125-2)

A twenty-one-year-old man was told about a life in a position of
power in Peru. Cayce was terse in citing cause and effect: "much *blood*
was shed. Thence anemia." He added that this soul had learned "that
service brought contentment, where power only brought dissension."
(4248-1)

A young boy with asthma was told that "one doesn't press the life
out of others without at times seeming to have same pressed out of self."
(3906-1)

A man struggling with increasing deafness was told not to "close the
ears, the mind or the heart again to those who plead for aid ... " (3526-
1)

A twenty-three-year-old woman asked what karma was causing her eczema. Cayce answered that the cause was "resentments in regard to those not thinking as self." (2872-3)

Sol Hambeing was the former name of a man now suffering with foot problems. He journeyed west in the gold rush of 1849 and gained much wealth but lost spiritually: "Not taking *from* [others] directly—but running over many to attain same . . . the feet . . . [have] brought much in of that suffered in *that* experience." (99-6)

Cancer

> *. . . each soul manifesting in the earth is the result of that the entity has been, in its use of its opportunities, in its relationship to God the Father.* 3121-1

Cancer is one of the most feared words in the English language. Although this reading begins by stating that this man's cancer is karmic, no past-life information is given. However, in his letter requesting a reading, he says that he was born with a tumor on his leg. An inborn illness is likely a past-life carry-over. The reading states that if he dedicated himself to God, he would find healing.

> . . . there are disturbing conditions. This disturbance is of a nature that by some would be called karmic. Hence it is something the body *physically*, mentally, must meet, in its spiritual attitude first; that is: as the body may dedicate its life and its abilities to a definite service, to the Creative Forces or God, there will be healing forces brought to the body.
>
> This requires, then, that the mental attitude . . . not only proclaim or announce a belief in the divine, and to promise to dedicate self to same, but the entity must *consistently* live such. And the test, the proof of same, is longsuffering. This does not mean suffering of self and not grumbling about it. Rather, though you be persecuted, unkindly spoken of, taken advantage of by others, you do not attempt to fight back or to do spiteful things; that you be patient—first with self, then with others; again that you not only be passive in your relationships with others but active, being kindly, affectionate one to the other . . . As oft as you contribute, then, to the welfare of those less fortunate, visit the

fatherless and the widows in their affliction, visit those impris-
oned—rightly or wrongly—you do it to your Maker. For, *truth*
shall indeed make you free, even though you be bound in the
chains of those things that have brought errors, or the result of
errors, in your own experience.   3121-1

Hypertension

*O what a jewel consistency must be in thine experience, if ye will
but take it and use it and apply it day by day!*   1537-1

In keeping with a central axiom of the readings that spirit is the life,
mind is the builder, and the physical is the result, Cayce gave very stern
advice about the attitudes of this thirty-eight-year-old man suffering
from organismic karma. The reading stressed that he had lived extrava-
gantly in many past lives and is still doing so.

> But if ye are attempting to have thy physical body doing just as it
> pleases, thy mental body controlled by "What will other people
> say?" and thy spiritual body and mind shelved only for good
> occasions and for the good impressions that you may make
> occasionally, there *cannot* be other than confusion!
>
> These . . . are not merely sayings; they answer to that which has
> been and is thy turmoil in the present. Look *within!*

Next, the Source hit the physical cause and effect hard. The man was
told that this condition would kill him if he did not mend his ways and
moderate his habits.

> Ye are sensitive to things about you; because ye have lived not
> only in this experience but in many others a very *extravagant* life
> in *every* phase of your associations with your fellow man! . . .
> Have ye not found within—as in thine own body in the present—
> that the extravagance of thy living has produced those very
> inclinations that arise in thy digestive forces?
>
> Thus thy high blood pressure that is produced within thy body
> arises from this overindulgence, this overactivity.
>
> And unless ye make reparation these conditions will overcome

thee. How may ye make reparation—by being what? *Consistent!*
O what a jewel consistency must be in thine experience, if ye will
but take it and use it and apply it day by day!

As to the material activities—keep away from those things that
hinder—such as the effects of alcohol, the effects of riotous living,
the effects of indulgence in those things that are of the nature of
great quantities of stimulations; whether they be in condiments,
excess of sugars, excess of this, that or the other. Or, as just given,
be *consistent!*   1537-1

Multiple Sclerosis

> But first the change of heart . . .   3124-2

> *And while to self in the present these conditions may not appear to
> be results of thine own self—whose body is afflicted?*   2994-1

Perhaps the most unique and personally overwhelming thing about
having a reading from Edgar Cayce was his uncanny ability to see right
into one's heart and mind. It was impossible to hide one's true thoughts
and feelings from his source. This man had two physical readings from
Cayce. He was not only crippled but nearly blind from multiple sclerosis. He was married and had a five-year-old son. When he was
diagnosed with this incurable disease, he attempted suicide.

There is correspondence about this case from the nurse who was
caring for this man. She was intrigued with Cayce's spiritual guidance
and remarked in one letter that "the most perfect body without spiritual development is after all, only a healthy animal!" (3124-1, R1) A later
letter from her showed how difficult this man was to help.

> The young man is an enigma to me though I have done much
> social work, and have nursed in a psychiatric hospital for a good
> many years. He has courage and good sportsmanship, but he is
> one of the most emotional and self-centered people that I have
> ever known. You say that I must help him to see that he needs
> spiritual food as well as physical help. I have tried, Mr. Cayce, but
> I don't think I have succeeded very well. He is touchy and close-
> mouthed, and will say, "Don't let's talk about it. It is too deep a

matter." I can't tell whether he feels a great deal, or not at all, except a burning desire to be physically whole again. We can't force a person to see spiritual values by talking about it. That is one reason I have assumed the responsibility of continuing to do for him, though his lack of consideration to me (and others who are trying to help him) and his egotism have nearly worn me out.

3124-1, R8

Cayce's reading for him cuts straight to the heart of the problem—his selfish attitudes. Since mind is literally the builder, this man's thoughts were blocking his body's ability to heal.

> ... this is a karmic condition and there must be measures taken for the body to change its attitude towards conditions, things and its fellow men...
>
> When the body becomes so self-satisfied, so self-centered as to renounce, refuse, or does not change its attitude, so long as there is hate, malice, injustice, those things that produce hate, those that produce jealousy, those that produce that which is at variance to patience, longsuffering, brotherly love, kindness, gentleness, there cannot be healing to that condition of this body.
>
> ... what would the body be healed for? That it might gratify its own physical appetites? That it might add to its own selfishness? Then (if so) it had better remain as it is.
>
> If there is the change in mind, in intent, in purpose, and the body expresses same in its speech, its acts, and there is the application of those things suggested ... , we will find improvement...
>
> But first the change of heart, the change of mind, the change of purpose, the change of intent...
>
> All of the mechanical appliances that ye may muster will not aid to complete recovery *unless* thy purpose, unless thy soul has been baptized with the Holy Spirit.
>
> In Him, then, is thy hope. Will ye reject it? ... Thy body is indeed the temple of the living God. And what does it appear in the present? Broken in purpose, broken in the ability to repro-

> duce itself! What is lacking? That which is life itself, . . . the
> manifestation of that influence or force ye call God . . .
>
> Will ye accept, will ye reject? It is up to thee.
>
> We are through—unless ye make amends. 3124-2

Here we have another case of multiple sclerosis. Sadly, this thirty-five-year-old man was told that even with a great deal of effort, he might only progress enough to be able to take care of himself. In keeping with mind as the builder, he, too, was directed to begin his physical healing by working on his attitudes.

> Now, while conditions are rather serious, they are long standing, and the condition has become progressive—we find that, with a great deal of care and patience, and persistence, the body *may* be able to care for itself—and to engage in activities that would be more in keeping with its purposes for its entering this material plane.
>
> First, the attitudes of the body must be considered. While at times there have been hopes, these have gradually faded; and the body has at many times become very antagonistic to all that would pertain to a spiritual or mental attitude that would be helpful.
>
> Resignation to the conditions does not necessarily mean patience on the part of the body. Know, deep within self, that God is not mocked. And while to self in the present these conditions may not appear to be results of thine own self—whose body is afflicted? Thy body is indeed the temple of the living God. What manner of worship hast gone on, then, in the *real* body? . . .
>
> For, each anatomical structure, each atom, each vibration of each organ, must be able to rebuild itself—if there will be the returning of the elements for its recuperation to any extent. There must be created—in mind, in purpose, in body—those influences and forces that will resuscitate life itself in each cellular unit of the body . . .
>
> That is the beginning then; thy attitude. 2994-1

Obesity

And too oft did the entity laugh at those less nimble . . . owing to their heaviness in body.   *1339-2*

With the growing obesity in our population, Cayce's advice to this seventeen-year-old student "to take self in hand" is good advice for all of us. We can see the hand of organismic karma in this case.

> . . . we find the entity was in the Roman and Grecian land, when there was the exchange of the games that were as part of what is now known as international or national athletic activity.
>
> There we find the entity excelled in beauty, in the ability to carry in figure, in body, the games that were a part of the experience.
>
> And too oft did the entity laugh at those less nimble of activity, owing to their heaviness in body.
>
> Hence we find the entity not only meeting same in the present from a physical angle but there are the *necessities* of it being worked out by diet as *well* as outdoor activity.
>
> Thus we find that in the present, from that experience, grace and beauty and the need for precautions become a part of what may be called . . . karmic forces.
>
> Hence the *necessity* for the entity often taking self in hand and applying will in those directions that will make for a growth in mental, material and spiritual development.
>
> For the necessity of such is a part of the experience of all, yet in the present experience for the entity—this entity—to enjoy the more of the material blessings as well as the personal satisfaction in being equal to others—it is necessary to take self in hand in those directions.   1339-2

Paralysis

The entity saw suffering, and the entity made light of same.

                                                          1215-4

Thoughts are indeed things. Again we see the role of past attitudes in this example of boomerang karma.

. . . we find the sojourn that is the more outstanding, as to the influences in the present.

It was during those periods when there were the persecutions of those who followed in the way of the teachings of the Nazarene.

The entity then was a Roman soldier, and one given rather to that of self-indulgence—and gloried rather in seeing the suffering of those who held to that principle.

And the entity fought in the arena and watched many that had met the entity fight again with the beasts . . .

The entity saw suffering, and the entity made light of same.

Hence the entity sees suffering in self in the present, and must again make light of same—but for a different purpose, for a different desire, for a different cause.

For again the entity meets self in that wished, that desired on the part of those against whom the entity held grudges. 1215-4

Parkinson's Disease

Not in that attitude, "I didn't cause it . . . "   *3100-1*

Sometimes it seems that the Source of the readings is being awfully harsh with the person who is ill. However, when we can view correspondence related to the case, we can gain additional insights about the person.

Elsie and Bill Sechrist became close friends of Edgar after being helped by their own readings. The man in the reading that follows, who was afflicted with Parkinson's disease, was a patient at Bellevue Hospital in New York when Elsie was a nurse there. She suggested that he get a reading from Cayce, and she later provided additional information about his situation in a follow-up questionnaire.

. . . I met him [3100] in about 1932 . . . and at that time, his condition was just beginning to show. As time went on, he got worse and worse. I was with Bellevue [Hospital] at that time . . . I was so thrilled with my own results from the readings and my husband's, that I talked to him about it and told him that I thought that this was a terrific opportunity for him; to get a reading and find out if there was an opportunity for him to be helped.

Whether it was a karmic situation or not, I didn't know . . .

(Q) Generally, what was his attitude towards life and pain? Would you consider him a spiritual man?

(A) No. He was so much of an introvert that there was very little discussion. But I knew from his attitude toward women that he was very sexually inclined, oversexed, as a matter of fact, and didn't seem to care too much about what he left in his wake.

(Q) After he got the reading, did you go over it with him?

(A) We went over it together.

(Q) What was his reaction to it?

(A) He was very hopeful. He thought that maybe something could be done for him. I went into, especially, that passage there about having to change and I tried to analyze with him: What is your attitude toward this, what is your attitude toward that, toward women, etc. But he seemed to be so reticent in exposing himself that I was sort of frustrated. I didn't feel like I could get to help him really in that particular angle. I know I told him over and over again, I said, "Now, [3100], judge yourself, analyze yourself, pray and meditate and see what it is that you are doing, or not doing, that you should do."

(Q) The last time you saw him was when?

(A) I saw him in New York in January, 1952 . . . He was in a pitiful state . . . [He was] very bitter. I think this may show something regarding this mental condition . . . He walks the streets, as he told my husband, and sends out thoughts of hate towards these other older people because he can't understand why they should be walking the streets, why they should be living, when his own mother was taken . . .   3100-1, R9

In this man's reading, the Source was hard–hitting and very direct. He was told that his soul chose to enter this body because he merited the condition.

> Thus, if there would be physical or material help, the body's first approach will necessarily be the study of self.
>
> Not in that attitude, "I didn't cause it," . . .

But rather consider that the self is being given an opportunity, here and now—if it will accept same—to interpret, to understand, and to be of help not only to self but in contributing something to the welfare of others in all their stages of development or seeking for physical, mental and spiritual help. . .

That there was the so-called *meriting* of this . . . understanding for this soul-entity, is indicated by the soul's choice and use of this opportunity for entrance into material manifestation.

Then, as you chose it, as you needed it, *do* interpret it properly.

Do not become one that finds fault with others, condemns others. For, know—as given of old—"Though He were the Son, yet even He learned obedience through the things which He suffered. . ."

Use those abilities of the mind in such measures and manners as to be ever a contributing influence for the creating of peace, harmony, love, kindness, gentleness, hope, in the minds and in the hearts of all with whom you come in contact day by day.

These are the first prerequisites if you would find help.

If you cannot accept this, forget it all. Do not even begin.

3100-1

Polio

And the entity laughed at those who were crippled . . .   1504-1

Here we see another person from the Roman soul group. This housewife also encountered boomerang karma. The reading hints that those around this woman in the present were with her in that incarnation.

. . . the entity was in the Roman land, during those periods when there were persecutions of those who held to the tenet of the lowly Nazarene.

The entity was among those of the royalty, being closely associated with the activities of Nero—and of those that were in authority during the experience—in the persecutions by the beasts with which men fought.

And the entity *laughed* at those who were crippled by such activities; and lo, they return again to thee!

How blest then art thou, that there are those close to thee that ye once laughed at; that are patient, that are kind, that are gentle with thee!

Then condemn not thyself. Rather know that ye are experiencing, ye are knowing that . . . ye may see the love of the Father manifested among the children of men!   1504-1

Some Contemporary Stories of Physical Karma

. . . spirit taketh form in mind. Mind becomes the builder. The physical body is the result.   3359-1

Steven Lee Carson, a longtime A.R.E. member and friend in Maryland, was very surprised when an X-ray revealed some unexpected, physical karma. About thirty-five years ago, his dentist became so alarmed when he looked at an X-ray of Steve's jaw that he sent him to a specialist for a consultation. Although there was no mark on his face, the X-ray showed a hole in his jaw about the size of a dime. The specialist said, "If I didn't know better, I'd say you had been shot." Thankfully, it was not cancerous, as was feared.

A few years later, a psychic told Steve that in a past life he had been a journalist in France. He had been murdered because someone thought that he knew too much and would talk. As a child in this life, he was so late in speaking that his parents took him to a doctor. Today Steve is a professional public speaker, journalist, and historian. He feels that the hole in his jaw may be the physical carry-over of a past-life wound, which also manifested emotionally in his childhood from the trauma of being shot for fear he would talk.

Ironically Barry Keener, an A.R.E. member from Georgia, experienced physical karmic pain while attending intuition conferences at the A.R.E. in Virginia Beach. During each visit, he experienced a pain between his shoulder blades within an hour of arriving in Virginia Beach. The pain would subside within an hour of arriving back home. After experiencing this for a couple of years, he wondered if it was related to a past life with someone at the conferences. Since he had previously found a hypnotic regression helpful in answering some questions, he scheduled another session to try to solve the back–pain issue.

While under hypnosis, he was asked to return to the time when he first experienced the pain. In a few seconds, he "saw" himself wandering the halls of a castle. When the therapist asked him what this had to do with the pain, he didn't know. The therapist then told him to ask if someone else in the castle knew the answer. When he replied that he was alone in the castle, Barry was then told to go back further to when the pain first started. Suddenly he "saw" himself on a battlefield, dressed in chain mail. He was fighting with another knight when he was hit from behind between the shoulder blades! When the therapist asked who had hit him, Barry "saw" the face of someone from the conference. The therapist told Barry that the reason the pain returned when he was around the person was that he had never forgiven him. They did a forgiveness exercise, and the pain diminished but did not go away completely. When asked why, Barry thought that there might be another person involved.

The therapist directed him to go back and find out if this was the case. Very suddenly Barry got very angry and "knew" that another knight from the castle should have been watching his back. If he had, Barry would not have been hit. When asked who this person was, again he "saw" the face of another conferee. Suddenly Barry told the therapist that he was feeling very guilty. He realized that he might have failed to watch their backs, causing them to be hurt or killed, and this was why he had gotten hurt. Barry and the therapist then did another forgiveness exercise, and the pain completely disappeared.

Causes of Physical Karma

. . . it is necessary that what we hate in ourselves or our associates become that we see in the experiences of life . . .   **288-37**

As we have seen, one of the threads that almost always appears in Cayce's health readings is the critical importance of the role that our minds play in both making ourselves sick and making ourselves well. This young mother was hemorrhaging from the throat and asked Cayce for help. He told her that her problem was not just physical.

In giving the interpretation of the disturbance here, other conditions than the pathological effects produced must be taken into
consideration—if there would be real help for this body.

That which is in the physical disturbing is, ever, the result of
breaking a law; either pertaining to the physical, mental, or
spiritual.

Here we have a misconstruction of some laws pertaining to the
physical and mental. Not as of morality alone, but the entity
should or must change the general attitude towards conditions
about the entity—its hates, its fears; and trust in those [spiritual]
promises that have been made.   3220-1

In another powerful example, the Source of the readings looked right
into the heart of the individual and the cause of her illness. Cayce told
this woman, who worked as an editor of religious publications, that she
needed to practice what she preached.

. . . these [problems] are wonderful experiences for this body,
even in the suffering and in the trouble—if the body will only
accept it as such. Ye have taught, ye have preached it in thy
literature and thy activities . . . what spirituality, practically
applied in the life of the individual, should create . . . if the mental
. . . is the builder of the body. Why not try practicing it in self?

The Source then tied these deep and penetrating observations right
into the multilevel cause and solution of her illness.

These are not harsh words, nor meant to be harsh, but the lack of
proper eliminations is the source of infection that causes arthritic
tendencies . . . [T]his should indicate to such a wonderful, a
beautiful mind as this entity, the lack of self-control, the holding
back in self of those things that should be stressed in mind, in
body. These are indications of the nature of disturbance in the
mental self, if the soul-purpose is in the right direction . . .

Then, in bringing about proper attunement of soul-purpose,
mind-activity, the body results should be creative and helpful,

> just as the attempt . . . to create that . . . for others. Can one teach
> greater truths than one practices in one's own life?   3395-1

In her next reading, this woman asked a question about past versus
present causes of her ill health.

> (Q) Is the ill health which I have been experiencing the past years
> the result of mistakes of a past life or is it due to something amiss
> in this present life?
> (A) Both. For there is the law of the material, there is the law of
> the mental, there is the law of the spiritual. That brought into
> materiality is first conceived in spirit . . . all illness is sin; not
> necessarily of the moment, as man counts time, but as a part of
> the whole experience.   3395-2

In a letter to Edgar, she shared the following insights about herself.
Clearly, she understood the connection between her mental/spiritual
life and her physical body. Her letter helps us understand Cayce's comments to her. Doubtlessly, many of us can relate to what she says.

> . . . four years ago I was just a "nominal Christian" and had no
> real deep prayer life nor sense of inner peace nor realization of the
> joys of the spiritual life and the service of others. I was full of
> doubts and conflicts and fears and I *know* I was making no
> progress then . . . There isn't much excuse for the years I wasted
> for I was always surrounded with Christian influences . . . Of
> course, all along I thought I was being a Christian but I didn't
> have the enthusiasm nor inner life that I have now. If I had all
> along had this, I'm sure I would not have the wrecked body I have
> now. But we can only go on from the place where we are . . .
>   3395-1, R1

In 1935 a member of Cayce's first spiritual study group asked a general but insightful question about the cause of physical karma. As was
so often the case, the Source offered stern words that are applicable to
us all.

(Q) Would the conflict between spirit and flesh cause one to be
affected physically, to become tired or even ill?
(A) *Relatively* so ... What was builded? ... something within self
which brought dis-ease ... [Something] at-variance to the divine
law! Hence it may truly be said that to be at-variance may bring
sickness, dis-ease, disruption, distress in a physical body ... O that
all would gain *just* that! and not feel, "Yes, I understand—but
... I didn't do it." Who else did?

This may be a hard statement for many, but you will eventually
come to know it is true: No fault, no hurt comes to self save that
thou hast created in thine consciousness, in thine inner self ...
                                                                        262-83

Cayce's axiom that *thoughts are things* feeds right into physical karma.
Whenever we hold strong emotions, we literally attract those things to
us.

For to all: Ye may meet thy Maker in thine own self. Hence it is
necessary that what we hate in ourselves or our associates *become*
that we see in the experiences of life, which will make for each an
understanding. For resentments of any nature bring their fruit in
the physical. Not that there should be wholly that of passive
resistance, but: *Thy will, O Lord, be done in and through me as
Thou seest I have need of for my soul development, and that I may
through this development be the greater channel of blessing to my
fellow man.*   288-37

In 1944 Cayce told this middle-aged woman that she was carrying
karmic problems in her body. His response to her question sheds light
on another aspect of the cause of physical karma. Not taking proper
care of our bodies, too, is sin.

(Q) Since all disease is caused by sin, exactly what sin causes the
colon and elimination condition?
(A) The sin of neglect. Neglect is just as much sin as [holding a]
grudge, as jealousy ...   3051-7

Let's not forget that good health and physical beauty are also karmic. A thirty-year-old model was told that her beautiful hands were the result of service from a lifetime in an English abbey. She had been a religious recluse who performed penance with her hands. The reading explained the cause and effect.

> And with the hands the greater labors were wrought.
>   . . . those activities then made for oft the toil, the trial, the unsightly work of the hands . . . where . . . there has been the service, where . . . there has been the expression of duty, love, patience, longsuffering . . . in a way . . . to bring about . . . the fruit of the spirit, [this] may be . . . seen in the . . . beauty in the hands . . . in the present.   1286-1

Hope in Physical Karma

There are in truth no incurable conditions . . .   **3744-2**

The spirit of the Cayce readings is ever hopeful. With mind being the builder of the physical, one's attitude makes all the difference in the results. The law of karma is ever operative, and this young woman suffering with paralysis was told that helping others might help her own healing.

> (Q) Is it possible that I will be completely normal?
> (A) Nothing is impossible. This depends upon the faith and expectancy of the body. Not that doubts don't arise, but more and more eliminate the doubts and use the body itself in administering good unto those not equal to the situations, and this may shorten the period considerable.   2968-3

The mother of a little boy suffering from epilepsy wrote Edgar about how much the child's first reading had helped him and asked this question from her heart.

> (Q) Is there hope for permanent cure?

(A) Are you praying about it? Are you living like that you would like for it to be? This is the answer! Is there hope? So long as thy faith in the divine cannot be shaken, there is hope! Life is the manifestation of God. He alone can forgive sins. Sin is in thine own surroundings as well as the entity meeting itself. There is hope.   3156-2

In an early reading from 1923, a question about the true nature of incurable illnesses was asked. The response was powerful yet simple and full of hope for all who suffer.

(Q) Is it possible to give information through Psychic Readings that will lead to the cure of diseases now known as incurable?
(A) It is. That which *is* was produced from some force . . . *that* [force] may be counteracted. The condition that exists in the physical bodies [are] all produced by conditions that may be met. There are in truth no incurable conditions . . . That which exists is and was produced from a first cause, and may be met or counteracted, or changed, for the condition is the breaking of a law, and the healing forces [must] become the compliance with other laws that meet the needs of the condition. The healing depends upon the individual, and the attitude taken toward conditions . . . As to the psychic forces, [they] only can give that condition that is . . . and the compliance with the law that may make a given condition. The whole rests then with such an individual . . .
     The evasion of a law only puts conditions off, and must eventually be met.   3744-2

The Source stated that there are no incurable illnesses. Illness is an effect and stems from a cause, and a cause can be counteracted. The key issue is that the real cause of illness stems from the breaking of a law. Healing comes when we are in compliance with God's laws. A psychic reading can provide the guidance, but it is up to the individual to engage his or her mind and will to make the necessary changes. We cannot put this off forever. We must all eventually meet the karma that we have created.

At the physical level, the key to understanding that there is always hope is found in Cayce's explanation that all the cells in our bodies are new over a period of seven years. Thus, as we work on ourselves, we can be a positive influence on the health of all those new cells. However, by implication, this is a long-term process. We must keep at it. Just as we did not get sick overnight, so we cannot erase the root cause of our illnesses overnight. Also very importantly, if as we begin to feel better, we go back to our bad habits, they will lead us right back to ill health.

> For the body renews itself, every atom, in seven years. How have ye lived for the last seven? And then the seven before? What would ye do with thy mind and thy body if they were wholly restored to normalcy in this experience? Would these be put to the use of gratifying thine own appetites as at first? Will these be used for the magnifying of the appreciation of the love to the infinite? 3684-1

The Source explained this seven-year healing process to a young advertising writer:

> For, as the very influences of the body are a growth day by day, so is the spiritual development a growth ... [I]n each seven years we are entirely new. Rather is it not true that *some* portion is new each day? It is a growth! For it is moment by moment, and not *wholly* cycle by cycle, that the change comes. 1597-1

Very late in Cayce's life, a woman with severe acne received a physical reading which stated that although "there are physical disorders ... The sources of these are not so self-evident. For these are karmic conditions and the entity is only meeting its own self." (5092-1) She never had a life reading, so we have no information about her past lives or missteps.

> As for scars, rather let the scars be removed from the mental and spiritual self. To undertake ... anyone altering these, we will have

worse scars. Let the scars be removed from . . . the *own mental and spiritual self*. Turn to . . . making application of the fruits of the spirit of truth; love, patience, gentleness, kindness, longsuffering, brotherly love, putting away those little tendencies for being "catty" at times or being selfish or expressing jealousy and such.

Let that mind be in thee as was in Him, who is the way and the truth and the light, and we will make the light of love so shine through thy countenance that few, if any, will ever see the scars made by self-indulgence in other experiences.   5092-1

Cayce tells her that having her scars altered surgically will only make them worse. He says that she must remove the scars from her mental and spiritual self by turning to the fruits of the spirit. If she does this, the reading promises that the light of her love will shine so much that others will not notice any physical scars that may remain from her past-life indulgences.

This forty-five-year-old woman was told that despite her suffering with paralysis, she still had much to be thankful for:

Don't feel sorry for self, but begin rather to see how much better conditions are for the body than for many another. Though the body itself may not be able to move as much or as easily as it desires . . . think how much better this is than no limbs at all, or those that are constantly in pain!   3642-1

From the higher perspective of the Cayce readings, illness is a consequence of sin incurred sometime in the past. This is simply cause and effect, or karma. However, even when a physical condition seems hopeless, the readings say that there is always hope. If the person who is ill can truly practice forgiveness, he or she will then earn forgiveness. This, too, is the law of karma. Like begets like. Forgiveness will lead to healing not only at the mental level but at the physical level as well.

Here, as we find, while conditions may appear as hopeless in the present; know there is forgiveness. Even as the body-mind may forgive others, so may the body here be forgiven. So may it seek

> through those promises of the All-Creative forces for help, yes;
> help in a physical as well as in a mental manner. 3504-1

In order to get the most out of a difficult situation, Cayce urged another man suffering with multiple sclerosis to practice patience and hold the following powerful attitude toward his condition: "The physical conditions that have come upon me are those most necessary for my own soul's development." This hard truth applies to us all. The reading continued by saying that this difficult situation had given others the privilege "to express in their activity the true spirit of love, that creative influence that is worshiped by man as God." The Source observed that these spiritual efforts and influences could help this man to renew his strength and reminded him that God's promises are sure: "Those that love Me will I renew . . . " (716-2) We can all gain hope and healing as we work with our physical karma by applying Cayce's advice given to this same man: Do your mental and spiritual work; recognize and appreciate the loving assistance of others; and have faith in God.

In summary, from Cayce's point of view there is always hope when dealing with physical karma. We are only required to do our work.

> To be sure, as it has been indicated again and again, there is that
> within the physical forces of the body—if it is kept in a construc-
> tive way and manner—which may be revivified or rejuvenated
> and kept in a constructive way and manner. This requires,
> necessarily, the proper thinking, the proper living, the proper
> application of those influences in the experience of an *entity* in
> its associations with everything about a body. 681-2

Ultimately, true healing at all levels is found through our attunement to the Spirit within, which is the source of all healing.

> The closer the body will keep to . . . [the] trust in spiritual things,
> the quicker will be the response in the physical body. For all
> healing, mental or material, is attuning each atom of the body,
> each reflex of the brain forces, to the awareness of the divine that
> lies within each atom, each cell of the body. 3384-2

For me, the Cayce readings have presented a comprehensive approach to working on myself, especially my physical and relationship karma. They offer hope, comforting counsel, and concrete suggestions that any of us can apply in our lives.

7

The Karmic Web–Our Relationships

*For each soul is as precious in the sight of the Creative Forces or
God as another...*   **3684-1**

Affairs of the Heart

If ye can't live very well with yourself—can ye with others? **5392-1**

"Marriage is give and take—mostly give." How many times over the years
I've heard my mother-in-law, Evelyn Jaffin, make that statement. And
she should know. She was married more than sixty-seven years to the
same man!

In many respects, marriage is the ultimate challenging relationship.
Two people could hardly be more enmeshed at all levels than a husband and wife—emotionally, legally, and financially as well as physically,
mentally, and spiritually. The Cayce readings say that it was Edgar himself in his Egyptian incarnation who was instrumental in the
establishment of monogamy. The human race has been grappling with
this arrangement with very mixed results for over twelve thousand
years. Many people came to Cayce seeking guidance about this most
important relationship.

A Good Marriage (939-1)

*. . . do not sit still and expect the other to do all the giving, nor all
the forgiving . . .*

In 1935 a young attorney and his fiancée received a reading from
Cayce in response to their request for mental, physical, and spiritual
guidance related to their desire for matrimonial happiness. Cayce not
only gave this couple a sunny forecast, he also provided wise counsel
that can benefit all couples, especially if they are consciously working
on building future good karma.

> . . . we have the enquiring minds . . . their desires, their hopes,
> and their aspirations. These . . . are well.
>
> If there will be kept within the intent and purpose of each *as*
> is the desire toward each in the present, well! For their minds,
> their bodies, their desires, are in the present in accord.
>
> Even though there would arise in their experience that which
> would . . . cause turmoils, dissensions, even strife, if their hearts
> and minds are kept—*ever*—in that of being a helpmate one for
> the other, such would become then rather as stepping-stones for
> greater opportunities, greater privileges.
>
> Should . . . either become self-centered, or allow selfish
> motives to make for demands one upon the other; or become at
> such times so self-centered as to desire the gratifying of self's
> desires irrespective of what the satisfying of same might bring into
> the experience of the other, then these would . . . divide the
> purpose. And a house divided against itself *will not* stand.

Essentially, this couple was told to hold fast to their present ideal of
each being a helpmate to the other. This attitude would lead them to
continued growth and happiness. However, selfish motives or desires
could cause their marriage to fail. Cayce's source then gave this young
couple some guidance that is similar to my mother–in–law's:

> Then, do not sit *still* and expect the other to do all the giving, nor
> all the forgiving; but make it rather as the unison and the purpose

of each to be that which is a *complement* one to the other, ever.

When they asked Cayce if their marriage would be a happy one, he said it was up to them to make it so:

> This, to be sure, is a state that is *made* so; not a thing that exists. For Life is living, and its changes that come must be met by each under such circumstances and conditions as to *make* the union, the associations, the activities, such as to be more and more worth while. Let each *ever* be dependent upon the other, yet so conducting self that the other may ever depend upon self. Thus will they find the associations, the mental forces, the spiritual activities that will bring peace and contentment in such a union.

And this advice was offered:

> ... they should each budget their time for their daily expressions, their daily needs, their social activities, their developments in the mental, in the material, in the spiritual welfare ...
>
> Leave the office in the office, when in the home. Leave the petty things of the home in the home, when abroad. But have all things in common.   939-1

Love affairs (971-1)

Indiscretions, and the sentiments ... based wholly upon material satisfactions, must bring the tares and the weeds in the experience of the body.

In stark contrast to the promise of the previous relationship, a young widow asked Cayce about a very different set of romantic circumstances.

> (Q) Regarding the two love affairs involved, please tell me what is best.
> (A) That the entity may find; not by just listening to what either of the men say. But first analyze in an equitable manner the whole situation; not considering self, but rather the promptings of the *inner* consciousness. Then pray over same. Take the

Creative Forces, God, into partnership with thee. And let the
answer then come from within.

If there is the consideration from the material or the financial
angle alone, or for self in this respect, such relations cannot help
but bring those things that do rust and canker; not wearing well
as the changes come about.

Approach, then, from the spiritual angle; and . . . it would
bring the more satisfactory conditions into the experiences of all
concerned.

His advice to her regarding how to make good decisions is very good
advice: Don't just listen to what other people say. Take the situation
within to your inner being and pray about it. Seek the Highest counsel
and the right answer will come. Making decisions from just the external
or financial angle will not hold up over time. Decisions which are based
upon spiritual considerations will benefit all concerned.

The widow continued to agonize over her dilemma.

(Q) Do you see that it is possible for me to straighten out this
tangled affair?
(A) *All* things are possible with God. Though it may bring some
heartaches, though there are already many regrets, begin with the
spiritual activity. Do not expect results in one day, nor one week.
Individuals do not sow one day and reap the next. They reap what
they have sown in the periods when *that* sown has come to
fruitage. For what ye sow, so shall ye reap. Indiscretions, and the
sentiments that are based wholly upon material satisfactions,
must bring the tares and the weeds in the experience of the body.

Those things sown in mercy, truth, justice, will bring their
rewards in the same realm, in the same coin as sown.

Cayce's reply is timeless and applicable to all relationships. First, she
is assured that the situation, no matter how messy, is not beyond hope.
No human tangle is beyond God's ability to heal. She must begin with
an attitude of spiritual intent and be patient if results seem slow to
appear. Like all of us, she will reap what she has sown in due time.

Indiscrete behavior will not yield good fruit. Only actions based in goodness will return goodness.

Marital problems (3292-1)

You only fail if you quit trying.

Cayce told the following woman, who was having marital troubles, that in her previous life her husband had bought her for a couple of pounds of tobacco! Her anguished questions and Cayce's answers provide many karmic insights and good advice for us all:

> (Q) Is it my fault that I am failing in every way in my home and marital relationship?
>
> (A) The entity is *not* failing. Do not condemn self. Condemning of self is as much of an error as condemning others. Live thine own self. Leave the results with God. Man may sow—only God may give the increase . . .
>
> (Q) How may I encourage my children in Christian thinking and living? . . .
>
> (A) . . . Live it thyself. Preach it little. For, what ye are speaks so loud, others seldom hear what ye say . . .
>
> (Q) What lesson am I to learn from my husband's unfaithfulness? Is it my fault?
>
> (A) Of thine own unfaithfulness in the experience before this . . .
>
> (Q) How have I failed to use wisely what God has given me? Why am I so confused about so many things?
>
> (A) Do not—do not feel that ye have failed. Do not judge self. You have not failed *yet*. You only fail if you quit trying. The trying is oft counted for righteousness.

Marital separation (1648-2)

. . . the letter of the law killeth, but the spirit of the law maketh alive.

Another woman asked a well-thought-out-question about her troubled marital situation, and Cayce complimented her on the question:

> (Q) What true relation does my husband [from whom I am

separated] bear to me and why did he come into my life? Can I
help him other than by good thoughts?
(A) This question — in relationship to husband and others for this
entity or any one soul — is well.

As has been indicated through these channels, there is never
a chance meeting, or any association, that hasn't its meaning or
purpose in the development of an individual entity or soul.

Then ... if any ... individual, takes a meeting, any association,
with the purpose or the desire to use same for self-indulgence,
self-aggrandizement, and no thought of the . . . development of
the soul for its purpose as it enters, then it becomes . . . *karma* —
[and] the individual becomes subject to *law!*

And . . . the letter of the law killeth, but the spirit of the law
maketh alive. Then the spirit of the law is exemplified in He that
is the Law of Love, and Grace, and Mercy, and Truth.

And they that use such associations, such meetings as such,
become helpmeets one to another — or stepping-stones for a
greater development.

Divorce (3179-1)
Any withdrawal entirely is the denial of obligations.
Cayce told this middle–aged woman that she had been "among the
chosen people journeying to the Holy Land," and "[i]n that experience
the entity suffered in mind, gained in principle and . . . patience that will
yet be tried as by fire." She was now meeting herself because she had
condemned others, and had also developed a pattern of withdrawing
from companionship because of "unbelief and unfaithfulness."
She asked if it would be best to divorce her husband.

(Q) Would it be a kindness to my husband and myself to get a
divorce? If so how soon?
(A) As to divorce, is one question. As to being apart and not
dependent upon the other nor interfering with the problems one
of the other is something else. Choose thou. Any withdrawal
entirely is the denial of obligations. Obligations are not set aside
merely by denial. But thy usefulness one to another has passed.

(Q) What caused my marriage to fail?
(A) It had failed before you began. These are karmic conditions.
The partner didn't measure up as well as thou hast.

Cayce told her that it was her decision to make but that one's obligations are not ended by denying them. He then told her that the relationship was karmic and that the marriage had been hopeless from the start. Marriage takes effort by both partners, and according to her reading, her husband had not done his share.

We should all be mindful of all of our relationships. All are purposeful; none are accidental. If we use our associations selfishly, they become subject to the law of karma and must be met tit for tat. If our associations are conducted in a helpful spirit, we will grow in accord with the purpose for which we incarnated.

I want to end this section on romantic karma with a contemporary example from Roberta Wirth, an A.R.E. member and biologist who lives in Minnesota.

Roberta writes that she is relatively new to the belief in reincarnation and stumbled upon the Edgar Cayce material only after having a past-life regression. As a biologist, she is very left-brained but sought the regression after being deserted by a man with whom she was in love and had a child.

At first, during the regression, she only succeeded in getting fuzzy images of being in a medieval dungeon with a dead baby.

But, on impulse, she asked a question about Jack London. She had had a crush on him since she was a child and had read many of his books. When the therapist asked if she'd known Jack London in a past life, her images immediately became sharp and clear and she found herself staring at a tree. It was an oak tree, and she could see every leaf and feel the dry, hot weather. Roberta also felt an overwhelmingly powerful feeling of love for London. She was crying and said, "We love each other." Jack London died in 1916 at age forty of kidney disease. When asked how she felt when he died, she replied, "Guilty, abandoned, grief-filled." Amazingly, the regression experience enabled her to heal her feelings for the man who had abandoned her.

Some years later, when on a family vacation in northern California, she learned that Jack London's ranch was nearby. When she took her young son there on a tour, she saw a large, old oak tree on the side of the cottage where Jack London had lived and died. The docent confirmed that the tree had been there when London was alive. She also noted that the air was dry and hot, just as she had felt it during the regression. She has been unable to dismiss this unexpected experience because it was so clear and powerful.

Ironically, as a biologist, Roberta's area of expertise is composting, and she later learned that Jack London used compost to rebuild the worn-out soil on his fourteen-hundred-acre ranch. Roberta has subsequently joined the Jack London Society, which is a group of scholars and fans, and she gave a presentation on London's interest in organic farming at their conference in Santa Rosa, California. She also learned that London and his second wife, Charmian, had a baby girl who died shortly after birth. Roberta wonders if she could have been Charmian. The two women share interests in music and art as well as travel and adventure. Charmian died in 1955; Roberta was born in 1956.

Parents and Children

Do not blame self; do not blame thy companion, do not blame God.   *5284-1*

The Cayce readings contain many cases that include complex karmic situations between children and parents. Often the child is seriously ill, and the parents face the responsibility, the challenge, as well as the growth opportunity of caring for the child. These karmic webs are learning opportunities for all concerned, even when there is little that can be done physically for the child. Cayce told the mother of a two-year-old boy that "conditions here are such that there are lessons to be gained from same, rather than so much that may be accomplished from a physical angle in the present." (3458-1)

A Child With Down Syndrome (5335-1)
Don't put the body away, it needs the love, the attention.
The following parents were told not to institutionalize this little girl, born with what was then called "mongolism."

. . . here we have an entity meeting its own self. These are not desirous and yet it is for the unfoldment and development of this soul-entity. Physically, only helpful influences may be brought for the mental and soul-self. Much may be the contribution for this entity in the present in kindness, patience, love. All of these are needed in the body. These will aid the soul. For, remember, the soul never forgets and that which is practiced to the soul, in the soul, will bring eventually a growth in the knowledge, in the understanding of the love of the Creative Forces.

Here we find an individual entity born not only to be a charge to the parents but it is needed for the parents, as well as needed by the entity . . .

Don't put the body away, it needs the love, the attention.

An Unhappy Pregnancy (3165-1)
In patience, in persistence, in love, find thyself.

The following case illustrates the complexity not only of familial relationships but also of our heredity. It is dramatic testimony to the power of our thoughts and emotions. In the letter requesting a physical reading for her eleven-year-old son, the mother stated that the boy was still wetting the bed. Two of her questions are very revealing and relevant to Cayce's diagnosis and recommendations:

> Why is he oversensitive, shy, and clinging to his mother, instead of looking for companionship of other boys, and instead of taking more interest in the life and things around him?
> Did his mother's unhappiness during the time of his expectation before his birth do him any harm?   3165-1, B1

Although Cayce stated that the boy had some abnormal pathology, the reading confirmed what the mother suspected. The cause of the problem was traced to emotional problems that "were received through the period of gestation." Apparently, during her pregnancy, the mother's attitude in some way made the "whole emotional body" of the child dependent upon her.

The Source stated that a past-life reading would offer a more com-

plete understanding of how the boy had attracted this physical condition to himself. However, since a life reading was not given, we cannot
know the past deeds or the past relationships. We are not told what past
cause led to the present difficulties.

The approach recommended by the reading was that the mother
make positive suggestions to the boy's subconscious mind each night
as he was falling asleep. This was to be continued for as long as necessary. The suggestions were not to be just about controlling his bladder
but should also contain guidance for his life's hopes and dreams. If
done properly, the reading said that this could transform the child's
entire mental outlook. However, it was very important that this effort
not be undertaken casually or done hurriedly. The Source warned that
if she did not meet this problem now, more difficulties would follow.

However, even before beginning to undertake this, Cayce told the
mother that she had some very serious spiritual and mental work to do.
She must first "find self." Although it would not be easy for her, she
must meet that which she created. The Source reminded her that this
child "has been committed to thy keeping, to thy care. It is thy problem;
not someone else's. It is thy boy of thy body, of thy blood, of thy mind."

> At first this may . . . be quite a problem for the mother. It will
> require the taking of self in hand, in meeting a condition that
> might have been controlled many years ago, during the period of
> gestation. For, as has been given, you must meet yourself; you
> must pay every whit . . .
>
> Find self. Know your own spiritual ideal, your mental aspira-
> tions for this body; and through the divine approach this body—
> daily, for a period sufficient to overcome the material conditions
> that disturb the body.
>
> Make those suggestions, as the body sinks to sleep, that may
> change the whole outlook, the aspirations, the desires, the hopes,
> the fears, the joys, the sorrows of this body.
>
> First, then, it must be within self; not merely as rote. But find
> self in this manner, in prayer, in meditation, to the divine; that
> self is willing, and then guide the mind and body. And make self
> willing! Meet the problem; else be responsible again for the

conditions that may come about in the physical and material experiences of the body.

As the body goes to sleep, give the suggestion not that it will merely refrain or that it will be able to contain or control the activities of the bladder and kidneys, but as to how its whole life in its hopes and its aspirations, may be guided—in its moral, its mental, its material aspirations . . .

These will do away with the doubts and fears. These will do away with those disturbances in the mind of the boy in his relationships with others . . .

In patience, in persistence, in love, find thyself. Then commit same in meditation, in prayer, to the real mind of this body.

An Unwanted Child (693-3)

. . . those attitudes and those wishes and those desires that made for the [soul's] entrance . . . have [brought] that which must be met.

Next, we have another sad and karmic case involving another eleven-year-old boy. This boy had epilepsy, was partially paralyzed, and was unable to speak normally. He often suffered convulsions when he was asleep. In addition to having two physical readings, this boy also had a life reading, so we have a great deal more information about his situation. His mother wrote this desperate letter to Cayce:

> [He] is in bed again and having convulsions every 20 to 30 minutes apart. He is so weak he cannot hold up his head or set up alone, but for only a few minutes . . . I am sitting by his bed. He was asleep just 15 minutes when he had a hard attack, and that is the way it goes, just as soon as he goes to sleep. Please tell me what I must do. I can hardly stand it any longer. I pray and pray, but it seems that I get no where. I am almost desperate. He has just had another while I am writing . . .
>
> I am handicapped so by not having finances or being able to go to work and leave him. I hardly know which way to turn.
>
> 693-2, R3

The child's life reading begins by noting that heredity and environment and family relationships are much deeper subjects than generally recognized. Souls are drawn together so that all can meet their karma. Unless the karma is met, the physical body of the incarnating soul will not be a healthy one. This very ill young boy was born in the same hospital in Washington, D.C., that I was born in, and since I incarnated with two inborn illnesses, this reading spoke deeply to me.

> . . . much . . . might be said . . . respecting heredity and environment. For these . . . go much deeper than ordinarily seen . . . Yet oft . . . individuals again and again are drawn together that there may be the meeting in the experience of each that which will make them aware of wherein they . . . have erred respecting experiences in materiality . . .
>
> For the soul lives on, and unless that which has been the trouble, the barrier, the dissenting influence in the experience is met in self's relationships to Creative Forces, it must gradually make for deteriorating experiences in the expression of such a spirit influence in matter—or materiality.

Cayce continued by saying that this boy's soul was influenced by physical and mental conditions that must not only be met by him but also his parents. Cutting right to the heart of the matter, the Source stated, "*This* soul, or this *body*, was not wanted" by his parents. Yet, since the parents' desires created the cause, the effect must be met. The Source chided all of us about the sacred nature of conception:

> O that . . . man would become cognizant of the necessity of preparations within themselves for being the channels for giving a soul the opportunity for expressions in the earth, or in matter!

The reading advised that conscientious efforts to apply the suggestions made in the two physical readings could, over a period of time, greatly help the boy. However, if these efforts were not begun soon, it would not be possible to heal the illnesses.

Knowing the boy's past lives helps us understand his present karma. In his previous incarnation, he had been in Salem, Massachusetts, dur-

ing the witch trials, when those who were experiencing "spiritual manifestations" were persecuted. He not only belittled those involved and
participated in their punishment, he took personal advantage of those
women in distress. He "used [them] in such a manner as to gratify, satisfy, the passions of the body." This then resulted in what Cayce called
"almost a possession . . . within the body." The reading explained that
when his mind attempted to rest, discarnate souls would creep close to
his consciousness and bring experiences of "uncontrollableness" to him.

Thus, when he slept, as his mother noted, he experienced disturbing
manifestations from those on the other side whom he had persecuted
and abused. Despite all this, the reading again offered assurance that
corrections could be made by his parents, who were responsible for
providing his physical vehicle.

Previous to his Salem lifetime, Cayce told him that he was in "the
Palestine land during the periods when the Master walked in the earth."
He was a scoffer and a member of the Sanhedrin itself, which was the
governing body of the Jews. The reading summarized this life as one in
which he "allowed self to be led away by that which seemed for the
moment necessary for the satisfying of the material expressions."

Cayce said that in another biblical incarnation, this boy had been
"among the first born of Jacob and Leah," into circumstances which
"might have brought . . . blessings":

> Yet when the desires of the flesh entered . . . [and] intolerance to
> [other] peoples, the entity made . . . associations that brought
> disorder, discontent within those of its own household and those
> of its people in that experience . . .
> These made for again those activities that have brought in the
> present the necessity of the awareness of the spiritual awakening
> within the expression and experience of the entity.

In yet a still earlier biblical lifetime, we can see similar patterns and
choices. He was among the "sons of Tubal-Cain when . . . polygamy first
began among those peoples." This brought what Cayce called "disorder,
disturbance, the unfavorable expressions of many about the entity; and
. . . experiences that have builded for disorders in the experience."

Sadly, this soul's patterns and past-life choices are very clear and very consistent; self-gratification was pursued again and again. The reading clearly shows that this soul had created the karma that it was facing in the present. Remember that this reading began with the warning that if a soul continues to reincarnate but does not mend its ways, it must meet itself in a weakened physical body.

At this point in the reading, Cayce indicated that he was ready for questions. However, when the boy's mother tried to ask a question, which the Source felt was missing the point of the message, she was cut off with this beautiful but final guidance:

(Q) Will he be given the power and—
(A) (Interrupting) This must be aided in . . . those manners as has been indicated. Follow those instructions. Make for . . . the constant prayer—not of a selfishness, but, "Show Thou, O Lord, the way to this erring soul, this wandering entity, that Thou may in Thine mercy bring harmony in the mental, coordination in the material with a perfect mental and physical body."
We are through for the present.

This contemporary story comes from Alma Verbunt, an A.R.E. member in the Netherlands. The insights she gained from the following experience helped her to better understand herself and to grow.

Alma met and fell in love with a man who did not return her feelings. In time, she felt better, but there still remained something that she couldn't put behind her. She decided to ask a shaman to make a trance-trip to gather information about this. According to the shaman, the man had been her child in a former life. The child had died even though she had taken good care of it. The shaman told her that the man's soul had appeared and had told her to tell Alma that she didn't have to feel guilty about his dying in that incarnation. He had decided to keep that particular life a short one, and it was through no fault of hers but by his own choice that he had died.

Alma said that like a hunchback, she had dragged that relationship around with her. The shaman healed her pain and it disappeared. Now not only did she understand her feelings about this man, she suddenly understood why she had chosen not to have children in this incarnation. With these new insights, Alma was free to forgive both of them and put this relationship completely behind her.

8

Some True-Life Karmic Tales

Experience is the only real teacher.   421-5

Apparently, karma has arrived in our mass culture. While working on this book, I heard a karmic story on the news! A woman in a Buffalo, New York, restaurant was choking on some food, and a man, who was washing dishes, performed the Heimlich maneuver and saved her life. They were both shocked to realize that seven years previously, this same man had been hit by a baseball bat and the woman had performed CPR on him and saved *his* life!

A Heart-Rending Experience
By Linda Schiller-Hanna[1]

For a long time, I've had an obsession with pyramids. For instance, in 1980, when I worked as a secretary in California, I had a picture of the Great Pyramid taped to my typewriter in hopes that daily visualization would help me manifest a trip I could ill afford.

A year or two later, I had a psychic reading with Sondra Ray, who led me on a guided visualization from the bottom to the top of a pyramid.

She had me visualize walking up the giant steps of the pyramid, each step radiating the colors of the rainbow through my feet as I ascended higher and higher. At the top, I was to visualize a healing experience with a man—we were both engulfed in pink light, representing unconditional love and merging—and then I was to go back down the stairs again, one by one. I felt a powerful shift with this exercise. Sondra encouraged me to practice it on my own each day to help secure my chances for true love. Because this was my dearest wish, I faithfully executed the exercise.

Earlier, in 1976, I had worked as a nanny for the Sterns family, and they had taken me with them to Mazatlan, Mexico, to help care for their children while on vacation. I fell in love with this beautiful ocean-side city, even though it had no pyramids. It was one of the most magical travel experiences of my life, and I vowed to return some day.

Later, I managed to take another vacation to Mazatlan, as I was then working as a secretary in Beverly Hills. I asked my travel agent if there were any pyramids in Mazatlan, and she assured me there were. Of course, I discovered after arrival that she was wrong, but I was directed by a knowledgeable native in Mazatlan to visit some small pyramids in Ixtlan Del Rio, a daylong bus ride away.

Since I had read some of the Carlos Castenadas books and remembered one called *Journey To Ixtlan*, I decided to take the bus and spend the night in this quaint little village. By chance, I arrived on All Saints Day, and within an hour of unpacking, the entire main street of the town shut down for a big parade. I joined most of the town's people in the square and then entered the cathedral for a special mass. Afterwards, being the only "Gringa" in town, not to mention being tall, blonde, and blue-eyed, I was surrounded by many villagers actively welcoming me to their charming, tiny town. I was humbled by this outpouring of love, and tears rained down my cheeks.

I asked them where the pyramid was, but they didn't understand my broken Spanish and pointed to the top of the hill. There was a large statue of Christ at the top of it, which they called Christo Rey, meaning Christ the King. I gaily asked a group of young, teenage girls to take me there, and they gladly helped me walk up the hundreds of steps and a steep hill to where the statue was. In my confusion, I thought it was the pyramid, but I later learned I was wrong. Finding a pyramid didn't seem as easy as I thought it would be!

The next day, someone told me that the historic Ixtlan pyramid was outside the town a mile or two and that there was no public transportation to it. Since I didn't have a car and there was no bus service, I decided to hitchhike there. I was given a ride by the town doctor, who treated me like gold. I sat on the pyramid and meditated, and he took my picture. This pyramid was quite small—about the size of a two-story building. I was frankly disappointed. I had hoped for something more impressive!

During this short vacation, however, I felt a strong pull to move to Mexico in any way that I could manage. I was totally enchanted by the country and her warm people, and I certainly wanted to know more about the pyramids.

Shortly after I returned to Beverly Hills, my parked car was involved in an accident. The insurance company paid me enough for my damaged car that I could afford to move there, and within a few weeks, I returned to paradise! I settled into a happy life in Mazatlan and worked in the resorts for several years doing psychic readings for tourists and local people. It was a good time for me and I thrived there.

Eventually, I fell in love with a local Mexican man who was attractive, educated, and sophisticated in many ways. He had been a city councilman, spoke impeccable English, and was kind and intelligent. We liked the same books and music, and we had a strong connection from the beginning.

Only one thing about him troubled me. There seemed to be a lot of other women after him, and he seemed to have trouble resisting these attractions. To say the least, my heart was broken several times during the course of our on-again, off-again relationship.

Despite a number of humiliations, I couldn't seem to get over him, and I went back to him again and again, often against my better judgment. I have since learned that when a connection doesn't easily break, despite difficulties and hardships, it usually means it is karmic and there is past-life work to complete, such as forgiveness!

Ultimately, he received word that he was invited to return to college in the United States to finish his degree in plastics engineering. As I was so smitten, I decided to return to the United States with him. While he attended school at the University of Lowell in Massachusetts, I re-entered American life. I learned to tolerate frigid, winter weather after enjoying three years of fantastic tropical weather.

Those were difficult months for me. He was constantly studying, and I was very lonely. I missed my friends in Mexico, and my family was on the West Coast. Worst of all, I happened upon a letter from a Canadian woman who had offered to meet him in Mexico on his upcoming Christmas holiday visit home. He had not told me of this invitation, and we had a bitter argument over it. I was not invited to go back with him and couldn't afford the trip on my own. He stubbornly returned to his homeland for the holidays, and I was left behind alone and profoundly distressed.

I suffered one of the darkest depressions of my life during the Christmas holidays of 1990 while he vacationed in Mexico. I went to three different church services, two on Christmas Eve, and one on Christmas Day, and invited a Chinese student to eat Christmas dinner with me. It was really a strange holiday! I sank into deep self-pity during this season while he was away, presumably seeing that woman. He asked to end our relationship, but I couldn't seem to give it up. I didn't trust him anymore, but I couldn't seem to leave or forget him either. I entered therapy and even had a joint session with him, asking the therapist to "help me hear" that he didn't want to be with me any more. The words didn't seem to sink in. I was stubbornly clinging. It was very disturbing. I almost felt suicidal. He finally told me directly: "Massachusetts isn't a big enough state for the two of us. You have to leave!" I was distraught but knew it was true.

This was spring 1990. I decided to move to Virginia Beach, Virginia, at this point and begin active involvement in the A.R.E. I really didn't know where else to go, and it seemed to be the right next step. We stayed in touch by letter and an occasional phone call. Finally, I asked him to come and visit me again, and inexplicably, he did. We shared another romantic weekend, which rekindled my hopes.

When he left on Sunday night without the promise of "lifelong true love," I was again in the bottom of a grief hole. I decided to take a hot bath, and I sat in the tub, crying my eyes out. Finally, it occurred to me to ask my spirit guides if the two of us had ever shared a past life together. I don't know why it took me so long to think of this, but it finally came to mind. Then I meditated in the bathtub and was given a vivid vision that I will never forget.

I saw this man and myself at the top of a pyramid near Mexico City, built by the Aztecs and known as the Pyramid of the Sun. I had actually visited it a couple of years earlier and been amazed at the ease I felt in climbing to the top of it, despite its ruggedness and height. That pyramid seemed very familiar. And no wonder! In my vision, I saw myself taking a huge knife, then cutting my boyfriend's heart out of his body and feeding it to the sun god. Then I threw his carcass off the side of the pyramid, which was meant to ward off disasters such as crop failure. I saw myself as a priest, and him as a slave being callously used for sacrifice. I was horrified and thought, No wonder he always seems to want to stay away from me.

I then thought, It makes a kind of sense . . . I cut his heart out physically, and now he's cutting mine out emotionally. After the vision in the bath, I called him up and told him about the vision and asked his forgiveness. Fortunately, he forgave me on the spot, and it was the beginning of the gentle and gradual finalization of our relationship. I could finally accept why he didn't really want me. I could finally let him go.

The postscript to this story took a whole year to piece together. I failed to make an obvious connection for many months. I had been born with a congenital heart defect. Some thought it was because my mother smoked during pregnancy; others thought that it was a genetic trait. I was born with a heart murmur, and doctors suggested I have open-heart surgery at the age of five. It was very rare surgery in those days, and I was one of the first to receive it. Although the surgery now involves just a small incision over the breastbone, they did it differently in the 1950s.

My surgery was done by taking a knife and cutting from the middle of my back, under the left arm, and ending under the breastbone in front. I was practically cut in half! I still have a huge, angry scar halfway around my body. My scar is quite visible, reddish, and spreads out broadly. It has been a source of embarrassment for most of my life, especially when I was a child.

I suddenly thought, Oh, I get it. Since I cut out other people's hearts in a former life, I had to have my heart almost cut out in this life to even the score. It explained why I felt such an attraction to Mexico. I needed to find this man and make amends to stop the cycle of karmic debt. I understood that the Aztec priests truly felt that this was the only way to save the whole civilization from certain collapse by famine or plague. Superstition ruled the day.

Although the cause–and–effect connection that I experienced cannot be proved, I feel a kind of peace about it now. I understand why my desire to move to Mexico was so compelling and why I had to have the surgery. And it made sense why this partnership failed to mature as I had hoped.

Later, when I learned from Henry Bolduc how to conduct past–life regressions and began to work with clients who had their own past–life– and present–life health issues, it became a complete circle for me. I no longer marvel at the wondrous ways God brings us to our healings. I marvel at how many people still resist the possibility that He can and will do it!

Karma—A Cosmic Wake-Up Call
By Dr. Joan Hanley[2]

"I think all of this talk about karma and past lives is unnecessary if our goal is to live a balanced and fully realized life," remarked a sweet lady in my Sunday morning spiritual development class. "All that you really need to concentrate on to make this life work, as well as the next, is to live love." I thought about her remark all the way home. Having worked on many facets of spiritual development for many years, I agreed with her conclusion wholeheartedly. Holding a sense of connectedness and love to the people and situations in my life is the most satisfying, growth–producing, yes, practical way for me to live, no matter the circumstances. I know "living love" is the highest universal law. The days that I keep this spirit/mind harmony are the kind I love to live.

However, the paradoxical thought that her comment prompted was that I might never have gotten to this realization had not karma—*my* karma—jolted me out of one life path thirty years ago and set me down on another, without the option of turning back. I didn't think of it as karma then. To me, God, after being my friend and protector, had abruptly withdrawn His favor and allowed my little family to be exposed and decimated.

There were challenges in my early years, a failed marriage and single motherhood, but the love and closeness of my two sons (then eighteen and twenty) had been both motivation and reward. I had two degrees, and a job I enjoyed in the school system. I was a traditional Christian whose vivid salvation experience had tapered off to trying to live a "good" life, expecting that God would look after me and mine, and saying an occasional prayer when I felt the need. There was very little vitality in my spiritual life, although I tried many churches, looking for "something" I couldn't quite define. As it was, my job and my little family brought me great satisfaction.

Then, in one instant, before dawn, a policeman standing on my doorstep changed me forever with these words: "Your son, John, was killed in an automobile accident early this morning." I felt a pulling sensation—like John was being wrenched from me, a door slamming in my face—and then nothing but the same three words, heard over and over, "John was killed," while somewhere in the distance my other son, Michael, was cursing and crying softly. I believe now that this event reflected a karmic pattern I had created in an earlier lifetime and lovingly was being given the chance to experience from a receiving perspective in this lifetime to learn from and to release. At that time, such a radical thought couldn't have been further from my mind.

There was nothing in my mind but those same three words, "John was killed," followed by my inner scream, No! in an endless cycle. My mind would not allow them to process but held them at bay, trying to expel them, trying to force open that door that had slammed on my son and find him. I didn't know that I was in shock, a protective altered state, which actually helped me to be receptive to the first guidepost on the new path on which I had landed, provided by none other than the son that I mourned. Having been told we should not and could not see John, Mike and I proceeded to the accident site, which had been swept clean. As I gazed numbly at the few small remaining pieces of metal, from inside my head came John's voice calling urgently and clearly:

"Ma! Get my glasses!" Pointing to the debris, I instructed Michael to get his brother's glasses, and there they were, twisted and broken! "How did you know?" asked Mike. "John told me," I mumbled, sliding back into the relentless litany of the policeman's words. Later, holding the glasses, I remembered the incident and wondered how it could have happened.

On my new life path, I've met many people who have had a similar experience—a sudden loss, or setback—which has forced them to reexamine the belief system they had relied upon to make their lives work. Something unpleasant or painful jars them. Then, when they are ready, a clue or a teacher appears. From seeming chaos, a new sense of order begins.

Such was the case for me when, a few days later, a book arrived in the mail, which John had ordered from an occult book-of-the-month club he apparently had just joined, titled: *The Miracle of Psychic Power: How to Pyramid Your Way to Prosperity* by Al Manning. I have since read the book, but that day it was completely alien to my way of thinking and I tossed it aside impatiently. A set of tarot cards came a week later, and still later a book of biographies of famous psychics arrived. Neither dented my skepticism, which was fueled by many stories about the dangers of getting involved with the "occult." What was my son thinking to have ordered these dangerous and kooky books?

Still, I was pursuing a mother's questions that would dominate all others: Where was John? How could he talk to me as though he were standing beside me? Was he all right? Was he suffering shock at the horribleness of his death? My church and the Bible had no answers to these questions. Maybe, I thought, there actually was someone—perhaps a Christian psychic—who had a reputation for honesty and been scientifically proven, that could shed light on what happens to people when they die. I found streets of gold and pearly gates a strange heavenly scenario for my motorcycle-revving son, and personally, I hadn't been impressed with that description of the afterlife either. Maybe that's why I had visited so many churches.

Suddenly finding out about the hidden, spiritual side of life, far from being an afterthought in a busy life, became all-important to me. I found the name Edgar Cayce in my search for a "Christian" psychic, and his biographies: *The Sleeping Prophet* and *There Is a River*. I visited Cayce's

Association for Research and Enlightenment, in Virginia Beach, Virginia, many times, where I found his fourteen thousand–plus readings and helpful guidance from teachers like Everett Irion and Shirley Winston. I formed a Search for God Study Group to study the readings and find support in living them. Hugh Lynn Cayce's *God's Other Door* and Raymond Moody's *Life After Life* answered many questions about my son's continued existence and eventually helped me achieve a sense of peace and divine purpose in his life and in his passing. My own life began to expand to include a growing familiarity with my spiritual dimension and awareness of divine order.

It didn't occur to me that such a thing as karma was expressing itself in my life in a powerful pattern until after the death from cancer of my older son, Michael, twelve years later. Even though I had an understanding of the process he was going through, and even though he had come to accept his passing, losing my dearest and truest friend left another enormous hole in my heart. Mike's final moments reflected a grace and triumph as well as a concern for those he was leaving behind, which left me in awe: "Mom, we all die. This isn't a big deal, you know. I've gotta go," his face lighting up. "They're waiting." That morning, John had come in vivid color in a dream, smiling his toothy grin and turning somersaults in an impossibly green field. Came to get his brother, I thought later. But then, Why did they both have to go? Slowly, an awakening to something half–remembered, something just beyond my conscious awareness came. Are my sons telling or showing me something?

I went back to the Cayce readings and Bruce McArthur's book, *Your Life: Why It Is the Way It Is and What You Can Do About It.* I had several past-life regressions. In one I was a young mother who chose to leave her difficult life and abandoned her young child. Then I remembered that my dad's mother, Myrtle, had died young, leaving a spoiled, fun–loving son in the hands of a stern grandfather, who worked him hard and boxed his ears when he felt like it. Mother had told me the story to help me relate to my father, who had gotten ever more withdrawn and taciturn as he aged. I began to imagine the young boy with no one to turn to and felt admiration for his steadfastness in a long, hard life. Could this be where it had begun generating a karmic pattern of opting out of difficult situations? I decided that it was an interesting possibility, but certainly not provable. Then I was faced with another instructive situation.

After Mother died, it fell to me to be my dad's full-time caregiver. "I don't want you here!" he snarled at me the day I moved in. "I don't want to be here either, Pop, but we're stuck with each other!" I replied, and began to shower him with the mother's love that had remained unused in my heart all of those years. Surprisingly, he stopped resisting me almost immediately, and in a short while he pronounced us "a good team." As Dad's health began to fail, I found myself taking on a mother's role and was glad to be the one to sit by his side. Was I finishing a job that I had started and then abandoned? Perhaps in some other time and dimension I'll know that answer. I do know that as my dad's life ebbed, a powerful sense of exchanged love passed between us, the feeling that all is well, and I felt the intuitive understanding that something else had come to an ordered close besides my father's life.

Looking at the family tree, I found that Myrtle's birthday was two days before mine, a situation sometimes indicative of a past-life link. But, in truth, my interest in discovering the source of that karmic pattern has faded away. Perhaps it has been resolved or at least its intensity lessened by my love for and service to my father. One outcome I know is that through confronting it, I have received healing for my sad heart and insight into how strong our creative powers are.

It's been over thirty years since I started over, from what was for me ground zero, for a belief system that self-destructed on the day my son John died. What I have come to believe is that God isn't out there somewhere, granting and withdrawing favor, as a human-designed deity would do, but is in all that is, including me. I have the potential within me to express His goodness and the freedom and the ability to use it to create beauty and life in this dimension in my own unique way, or not, as I choose. Some of the karmic patterns I've created by my choices are not helpful to me and others and need revisiting from a different perspective so that I may feel their impact and learn from them. What could be more fair?

Acknowledging and growing through experiencing our karma is "meeting self," as Edgar Cayce called it. A pattern of abandoning a young life, without regard for the pain of those left behind, needed to be experienced with me as the one left behind. My sons and I had agreed at the soul level upon this "lesson" this time for mutual learning. When the Bible says to "work out your own salvation with fear and trembling" (Philippians 2:12), I think that it is telling each of us to create our own best path home. This is mine for now. Someday I will realize my full God potential and be free to move beyond this dimension even closer to the God Source. The accomplishments that will count most are not just beliefs or intellectual mastery of concepts but realized expressions of God qualities, and these are the gifts I will bear.

While my mother's heart misses my sons, I know they are alive and on their own paths. I don't begin to understand the finer workings of the dynamic we went through together, but I humbly thank them for their part in it and for the growth and richness of the spirit it brought. I also wonder if I would ever have come to this path, this time, if they hadn't helped bring one of my karmic lessons to me as a cosmic wake-up call.

Lincoln's Secretary of War

An A.R.E. friend from New York named Joseph Korsunsky sent me this very karmic tale about a possible past incarnation.

Edwin Stanton was secretary of war under President Abraham Lincoln. He is widely considered to have been indispensable to the Union victory and was in charge of the pursuit, capture, and trial of Lincoln's assassin and the other conspirators. In personality, Stanton was regarded as harsh, vengeful, humorless, and unforgiving.

Joseph Korsunsky's lifelong identification with the Civil War period began when he was brought to Washington, D.C., by his parents as a tourist at the age of ten. Upon entering Ford's Theater, where President Lincoln was assassinated in 1865, he suddenly proceeded to pace off the assassin's movements in the theater and was enthralled by the whole atmosphere. Years later, it was discovered that a day or two after the assassination, Edwin Stanton had entered Ford's Theater and, despite his age, had also paced off the assassin's possible movements.

At the age of fourteen, Joseph and his parents drove to Florida, before Route 95 was built. They used Route 301, which was an undivided highway at the time. Upon entering a small Virginia town and before seeing any identifying signs, Joseph began to point out approaching landmarks before they were visible. The boy suddenly blurted out that he thought that this was where John Wilkes Booth was captured and killed. And it was. The town was Port Royal, Virginia, and the site marker soon appeared. (Joseph had always suffered from carsickness so badly that his father said that he could never wear a hat because his son was always puking into them. Although the boy was beginning to feel carsick as they approached Port Royal, the sensation abruptly ended and has never reoccurred in almost fifty years.)

When Korsunsky was in college, he met a Stanton relative and became his research assistant on a book while in graduate school in 1965. Their long conversations about Stanton made Joseph somewhat of an expert on the life of the secretary of war. He has often found himself defending Stanton, whose harshness, bitterness, secretiveness, and vengefulness made him a controversial figure. Lincoln was able to overlook how humiliatingly Stanton had treated him when they were both young lawyers working together on a case. Stanton felt that Lincoln was just a backwoodsman and called Lincoln "the original gorilla." All that changed once they were in daily contact during the Civil War. They became such good friends that the families took summer vacations together. Lincoln's son Robert invited Stanton to his wedding in 1868—the only cabinet member of his father's to be invited.

As an adult, Korsunsky is of the same height and build as Stanton. They apparently also share some unusual personality characteristics. In the 1970s, Korsunsky acquired an antique coffin, which he calls his "coffin table," that to this day is in his living room. Later, he discovered that Stanton also temporarily kept a coffin in his home, which was occupied by one of his children who had died.

Stanton's personality was formed in part by the many losses which he suffered, including that of his first wife, and his brother to suicide. It was Stanton who discovered his very bloody body. There is a story that when Stanton was younger, he was fond of a waitress in his rooming house. One day he was told that the waitress, who had served him that morning, had died and had already been buried. Stanton was so upset that he ran to the grave and proceeded to dig her up. Korsunsky, too, has had some eerily similar experiences. His wife committed suicide, and he also had the misfortune to discover a bloody body, that of a classmate who had blown his brains out.

Years after discovering the work of Edgar Cayce in 1972, Korsunsky had a psychic reading in which he asked, "Did I have a role in the Civil War, and if so, who was I?" The psychic replied that she did not know who the person was, but asked if he was familiar with the name Stanton. Soon she visibly shuddered, saying that this was too bloody and awful and, "Let's get out of this."

For Korsunsky, synchronicities involving Stanton continued. While being shown through the attic of a Lincoln site, which had just been acquired for public use, Joseph discovered a large, framed picture of Stanton. It now hangs prominently in the library. No other cabinet member's picture was ever found on the site. Later, when Korsunsky had the opportunity to sleep overnight in the historic site, he found it physically uncomfortable because it had not yet been restored. Late at night, he went into the library, pulled two wing chairs together, and fell asleep. The next morning he found that his head was next to a book-shelf upon which rested a numbered copy of a tribute to Stanton written by the site's owner. This was right next to the fireplace where papers, reported to incriminate Stanton in a scandal, were purportedly burned in a coverup. The presence of the tribute and the picture greatly contributed to the widely accepted belief today in Stanton's innocence in the matter.

9

Many Lives, Many Lessons

. . . no individual finds self in any position in the material world save by the grace of the Father-God.   *3474-1*

Cayce Readings in the Jaffin Family

Hence it is not merely coincidence or accident that their lives, or the personalities, are in the positions as they find themselves in the present.   *954-4*

In our busy, daily lives, karma can be very subtle and illusive, or it can be heavy, like the blow of a sledgehammer. The great psychologist Carl Jung coined the term *synchronicity*, which means a meaningful coincidence. For me, whenever I experience synchronicity, I pay attention. I consider synchronicity a likely hint that this event is important and has something to tell me. It could even be related to a past life and thus be karmic. In 1978 my husband and I had an experience that was as surprising as a sledgehammer, but its meaning is subtle and illusive.

Neither my husband nor his parents had ever heard of Edgar Cayce until they met me in 1972. Given my enthusiasm for Cayce's work, I dare say that over the next several years, they heard more than enough about him. My husband and I were not present at an out–of–state family gathering in 1978, when a wealthy cousin, whom my in–laws hadn't seen in many years, mentioned Edgar Cayce! I guess that their opinion of me received an unexpected boost. This branch of the family lived in New York and knew Edgar's best friend, David Kahn. Between 1942 and 1944, various Jaffin cousins had a total of twenty readings!

To this day, I feel the hand of karma in this amazing "coincidence," but I've never been able to get a good handle on what this all really means. In general, I feel that this very unexpected connection is somehow related to my writing this book. As I said right up front in my dedication, I couldn't have done it without my husband's support. Perhaps this meaningful coincidence helps to account for his sustained assistance as I have labored over this project for many, many months. Maybe it even influenced his soul's decision to enter in 1946. But whatever the full explanation, it has all been most interesting as well as a blessing and a gift.

Understanding My Karma Through Hypnotic Regression

No soul enters by chance, but that it may fill that it has sought and does seek as its ideal.   3051-2

In 1983 I began a holistic health program with Dr. Genevieve Haller and her associates in Virginia Beach to address my hereditary disease. Dr. Haller scheduled a wide array of therapy appointments for me, and I traveled to Virginia Beach to be worked on by an array of healers. This was a wonderful experience, which I feel has staved off the worst effects of my crippling illness. My father was on disability retirement and in leg braces at age forty–two. I have continued to walk unaided and have been able to travel the world well past that age.

However, I very much wanted a deeper understanding of this physical challenge with which I had incarnated. Cayce considered hereditary illness to be the pathway of karma, and I wanted to understand whatever I could about its deeper causes. It seemed to me that the best place to find the real cause of an inborn illness is in a past life. So Dr. Haller recommended Carolyn Gelone for hypnotic regression, and we had several sessions in 1984 and again in 1993. They were very meaningful and thought–provoking. I recently listened to the tapes again and discovered many additional valuable insights. In terms of my primary physical challenge, four past lives, which seem interrelated, stand out.

Unholy Self-Mutilation in India
   Thy body is indeed the temple of the living God.   3902-2

As a former geography teacher, I've always wanted to see the world and have been pretty successful. I feel very blessed to have visited over forty countries, often exploring very remote and physically challenging areas. Many of my trips were with A.R.E. tours. Despite my physical limitations, I've always been a hearty traveler and stayed pretty healthy despite all the stresses that world travel entails. The exception was a trip to India in 1990. Not only did I get sick, but the day after returning home, I had a fever of 105° and my doctor wanted to hospitalize me. Thankfully, this was not necessary, since my mother used an old remedy and broke my fever by rubbing me down with rubbing alcohol. I wondered if perhaps this unusual reaction was a clue to my having had a problematic life in India. It was through a regression three years later that I had an opportunity to explore this possibility.

In this Indian lifetime, I had been a sadhu—a Hindu ascetic. Apparently, I sat under a large tree meditating for many years. Local people brought me food and water. However, I seemed to have missed the point of spiritual practice. I was arrogant, judgmental, and condescending. I looked down on other people, even those who brought me food and water. I also disdained my physical body and considered it a barrier to attaining higher consciousness. I even went to the extreme of self-mutilation by pushing thorns into the muscles of my arms and legs, especially filling my calf muscles with them. I certainly did not love and care for my body temple.

This brief recall provided a couple of clues to my present life. Despite my dedication to spiritual disciplines and long years of deprivation in that life, I missed the spirit of Spirit. My attitude toward my fellow man was very unloving. In my present life, I've always had an interest in the mystical, which helps us nurture love for other people. My mutilation of the muscles of my limbs may well translate into part of my present problems. Today very tight calf muscles are one of my greatest impediments to normal walking. I do exercises to stretch those muscles many times each day. I feel that my subconscious mind remembered a life in India of both physical and mental error. No wonder visiting India made me sick.

Knee Karma From Spain

> *(Q) Have I always incarnated as a woman?*
> *(A) No. Only those as women have been given, but you've been a man.*   3051-2

In my present life, I joke that I'm domestically challenged and that I can blame a past life! As they say, I don't do windows. But I also don't do floors or certain other household chores. And my knees are a big part of the reason. For many years they have been painful and problematic. They scream in protest if I get down on them. So I don't. I found the origins of my knee pain and my distaste for domestic drudgery in one of my 1984 regressions.

I was a woman unhappily scrubbing tile floors, probably in Spain. I was dressed in a long, dark dress that had once been nice. I don't know if it was my last dress or a hand–me–down from the family I worked for. I knew I was a distant relative of the owners of the ranch or hacienda where I lived, but that didn't matter. I had fallen on hard times, and they gave me a roof over my head as long as I worked as hard as all the other servants. I had no children and didn't know where my husband was. He had been gone for years, perhaps fighting in a war or dead.

I looked out a window and saw a dry landscape with low mountains in the distance. There was a group of six or seven men riding off on horseback. Oh, how I longed to be free to ride off with them and never return. But women didn't do that. I longed to be a man; I longed for freedom.

A Mongol Warrior

> *. . . sex change is more from desire than from* physical earth-
> incarnation's influence . . .   311-3

As the readings say so many times, thoughts are things. I got what I had longed for in my next lifetime. Not only was I a man, I was on horseback! Specifically, when Carolyn asked me to go to the lifetime that was the source of my physical problem, this powerful experience emerged.

I came into that memory on horseback, riding hell–bent for leather. I was in the forefront of a small group of Mongol warriors who were pursuing defeated foes. I could feel the blood lust; it was actually visceral. I wanted to get them and kill them all, even though they were defeated and fleeing. I felt no mercy, just as disease has no mercy.

As Carolyn and I explored that lifetime, I saw myself in battle totally focused on victory. Genghis Khan is reputed to have said, "Man's greatest joy is to crush his enemies and have them flee before him . . . "[1] I seemed to have taken his policy to heart. My horse and I were covered in blood, and we trampled others underfoot, even if they were still alive and crying out for help. I went on to rise through the ranks and was recognized by my khan for my prowess in battle. I had a family back home, far away, but they were of very little interest to me. My wife gave me sons and that was all that mattered. I didn't see them for years at a time.

Now, over twenty years later, I can still feel the emotions of that experience when I think about it. I was shocked at my own brutality but felt great relief that I've moved beyond that mentality. I literally ran roughshod over people who were suffering, and I've been brought down to Earth by my own body. I still love horseback riding, but because I lack good leg strength and balance, I will never be able to freely gallop a horse, as I'd dearly love to do.

A Trader on the Silk Road

> *. . . for all who take the sword will perish by the sword.*
>
> *Matthew 26:52*

Again I was drawn back to the vastness of Asia. This time I was on foot. This pivotal past life revealed my karmic connection to my father. I was a trader on the great Silk Road, which was a network of roads connecting China and other parts of the Orient to the Mediterranean world. I walked thousands of miles over the mountains, steppes, and deserts of Central Asia, usually alone with only a pack animal. I dealt in small, valuable, easily transportable goods. This was probably during the fourteenth–century Pax Mongolia, the peace imposed on much of

Asia by the Mongol Khans to promote trade and communication. I had been warned by friends to always travel with a caravan, but I was stubborn and willful, and I paid with my life. I was ambushed and murdered by a small group of Mongol soldiers, and of course previously I had been a ruthless Mongol soldier myself. I remembered thinking to myself that they were supposed to protect travelers, not murder them. When Carolyn urged me to look into their eyes to see if I knew them in this life, I recognized all five—among them were my father, my father-in-law, and my previous husband! In both Asia and America I have reaped what I have sowed.

Karmic Patterns

. . . no contact, no acquaintance, no friend, no—not even a foe or a passing acquaintance is without purpose . . .   1404-1

These are just a few of the past lives that Carolyn and I identified. They provided a wealth of clues and insights into my deeper self as well as my present-life circumstances. As the callous and violent Mongol, who literally rode over other people, it certainly seems that we found the main cause of my hereditary condition. Other Asian patterns were also identified. I've always been attracted to the wilds of Asia and have traveled to those areas several times. I read Harold Lamb's biography of Genghis Khan when I was twelve years old and still love to read about the peoples and history of that remote part of the world.

Not only did Carolyn and I find mundane things, like why I so dislike housework, we found other patterns that echo in my present life. One of the obvious themes in these four lifetimes was dependence versus independence. Obviously, as the Spanish woman, I was totally dependent on family charity for the very roof over my head. In the three male lives, I was extremely independent. My streak of stubborn independence even got me killed on the Silk Road, because I ignored warnings and traveled alone. Perhaps of greatest importance, in none of these lives was having a family very important to me. In India I was an ascetic; in Spain, childless and probably a widow; as the Mongol, my distant family was irrelevant to my life's goals; and when traveling the Silk Road, I was unmarried. Now as a woman again, family ties are very important to me, but they are often challenging. It seems like a karmic clue that, given the muscular problems in my extremities, the finger that causes me the most discomfort and difficulty is the finger on which I wear my wedding ring!

Karmic patterns are like recurring dreams. Our unconscious minds, which never forget, have important messages for us and try hard to get our attention. If you discover recurring patterns in your life, they may well be carry-overs from past lives that need addressing in the present. We certainly don't want to keep carrying them with us into our future incarnations. In the next part of this book, we'll examine some of Cayce's most important suggestions for healing karma and moving forward into grace.

Some Additional Hypnotic Regression Stories

Lucy Dickinson, an A.R.E. member in Arizona, sent me a couple of personal examples of hypnotic regression as an aid to healing. She had a fear of being in tunnel-like structures. During a hypnotic regression, she went back to a very traumatic life as a holocaust victim. She saw herself standing on the edge of a pit and being shot in the back of the head. The shot glanced off her head and wounded but didn't kill her. She fell into the hole and was buried alive with other bodies. All her life, she had dreams of her mouth filling up with sand and dirt. These dreams came mostly during times of stress. Since the regression, she's had no more of these dreams and no more problems with tunnel-like structures.

Lucy had another regression that dealt with that same time period. She was one of the children who were experimented on and given medications. In her present life, she's had a great deal of difficulty taking medication. After another regression, she is now able to take medications.

Carolyn Gelone, who conducted my regressions, is a former A.R.E. staff member now living in Pennsylvania. She has also benefitted by being regressed and shared this personal story of release from physical karma. At ages twenty-one and thirty-five, she tried to wear contact lenses.

Both times, she experienced a bad reaction of red eyes, irritation, and general discomfort. Each time, the doctors assured her that her eyes were fine. This meant that the physical structure of her eyes was normal and that she had enough tear production to wear the lenses. Yet the symptoms persisted.

At age forty-two, she was determined to try again to successfully wear contacts. She realized that if her physical eyes were fine, then the problem must be psychological. She went to a hypnotist, before buying the lenses, and asked him to make her a tape to program herself to receive the lenses. The tape told her how comfortable the lenses felt in her eyes and how wonderful it was to wear them. Carolyn was very dismayed when she got all the same symptoms—red, irritated eyes and general discomfort—while just listening to the tape!

Being a past-life regressionist herself, she knew that the problem was deeper than just a psychological issue. She decided to explore a past life to look for a hidden cause of the aberration she was experiencing. What she found was a life in which her eyes had been put out by wooden stakes. It hadn't killed her but it blinded her for life. Carolyn realized that her eye memory, or pattern, was, "If I put something in my eyes, I'm going to go blind." Her reaction was an outdated protection pattern.

It was now time to update the pattern. She explored the details of the past life and released the triggers from the outdated pattern. The result was that now in this life she is able to comfortably wear contact lenses!

Kathleen Peters is an A.R.E. member and hypnotherapist in Kentucky who also shared some regression experiences. In a Chinese life, she was murdered by her son. He was a warrior and could not go to battle as long as he was responsible for her. She was not angry with him, because she understood that he needed to fulfill his destiny. But even in death, she felt that she needed to remain close to him, and so she followed him into battle, where he died shortly afterward. When his spirit left his body, he was shocked that her spirit was still with him. She told him that they needed to find the light together.

In this lifetime, Kathleen found the roles reversed. Her son returned as her mother and introduced her to reincarnation, but Kathleen promptly discounted the idea. Kathleen regrets that she did not give her mother credit before she died. Sometimes her mother comes to her at night in the form of sensations in her toes or feet. When she speaks to her mother, the sensations immediately stop. This frequently occurs at 4:44 a.m. Kathleen became certain that it was her mother visiting when she realized that if she turned the numbers upside down, they were her mother's initials—hhh. In addition, when Kathleen checked her birth certificate, she found that her time of birth was 4:44.

Kathleen also found regression helpful with her fear of animals. Previously, she would walk around the block to avoid even the smallest pooch. A regression placed her in a primitive life as a black man in Africa. A wolf had been threatening the tribe. One night it came and killed a baby. As the largest and strongest tribe member, she was chosen to go kill the wolf. Kathleen reports that she was terrified but successful. However, when she returned, there was a celebration that included a "fun fight" with knives in which she was accidently killed. After the regression, her fear of dogs and animals disappeared. Her family was shocked to see her petting and enjoying cats and dogs.

Part III:
Spiritual Alchemy– Transforming Karma Into Grace

[The entity meets] those things which have been called karmic, yet . . . under the law of grace this may not be other than an urge, and . . . making the will of self one with the Way may prevent, may overcome, may take the choice that makes for life, love, joy, happiness—rather than the law that makes, causes the meeting of everything the hard way.   1771-2

What ye sow, ye reap, unless ye have passed from the carnal or karmic law to the law of grace.
   Then know that whatever exists is for a purpose, for He having overcome the world may aid thee in overcoming the world.
                                                                      5075-1

. . . it is a fact that a life experience is a manifestation of divinity. And the mind of an entity is the builder. Then as the entity sets itself to do or to accomplish that which is of a creative influence or force, it comes under the interpretation of the law between karma and grace. No longer is the entity then under the law of cause and effect—or karma, but rather in grace it may go on to the higher calling as set in Him.
   Keep the faith in the Lord, not in things.   2800-2

10

Grace Comes in Many Forms

For, it is by the grace and love as manifested in the law of Creative Forces that an individual entity experiences life in a material manifestation.   *2905-3*

What Is Grace?

The law of the Lord is perfect. His grace is sufficient if thy patience will be sufficient also.   *5001-1*

Ultimately, grace is a mystery. In his Epistle to the people of Ephesus, St. Paul tells us that, "For by grace you have been saved through faith, and . . . not of yourselves; it is the gift of God." (Ephesians 2:8) The dictionary defines grace as "unmerited divine assistance given man for his regeneration or sanctification."[1] It is difficult to conceive of such unmerited generosity. Although the full grasp of all that grace is may be beyond the comprehension of our physical, three-dimensional minds, we can hardly fail to see the myriad manifestations of God's grace all around us each day. It is part of us in the miraculous bodies that we inhabit, and it is all around us in the beauty of nature.

Cayce explains that the path of grace, which each of us may follow, will allow us to become conscious of our inner divinity. This awareness will grow as we take the necessary steps to transform our karma into grace.

For, with each life experience, each entity is shown grace and mercy by a divine justice. For, He hath not willed that any soul should perish, but hath with every temptation offered a way, a means of regeneration of activity in which the soul may find its relationship to the Creative Forces.

Hence this is the purpose for which ye sought thy experiences in interims between material manifestations, as well as the earthly sojourns.

These indicate that there *are* virtues as well as vices. *Magnify* the virtues, minimize the vices; that ye may know—truly—that thou hast in thyself that which will, which may, which can, awaken to the divine within each manifested soul in a body.

                                                                                            2410-1

We can take comfort from the thought that whether or not we recognize it, each of us receives grace and mercy in every lifetime. Remember, the readings say that the statement that God hath not willed that any soul should perish is the truest statement in the Bible. This is grace indeed.

Here is how we transform our karma into grace. It is simple, but it can also be very challenging. Cayce's instruction is to magnify the virtues and minimize the vices. We can do this within ourselves by honestly examining ourselves and seriously pondering the key concept that with *every* temptation, God offers us a constructive way out of our difficulties. No matter how dead-end or desperate a situation may appear, there is always a better choice or a higher response that we can make. It is up to us to call on our God-given free will to make the better decisions and to take the necessary steps to move away from our counterproductive habits and habitual responses, and nurture and build on our strengths at every opportunity.

We can also magnify the good qualities of other people in our thoughts and interactions while minimizing their faults. Although we may not be able to perceive any external difference in the problem after we do this, Cayce assures that our efforts move us forward toward a higher consciousness. And this spiritual maturation is the very purpose for which we were created and for which we reincarnate over and over again. Both of these approaches will help us to see the divinity in others as well as in ourselves.

How May We Know Grace?

... overcoming [karma] must be a continuous practice in the daily experiences with others.   *2329-1*

The tools that we need to move from karma into grace are what the Bible calls the fruits of the Spirit. St. Paul lists them in his Epistle to the Galatians:

> But the fruit of the Spirit is love, joy, peace, longsuffering, kindness, goodness, faithfulness, gentleness, self-control.
> Galatians 5:22-23

Cayce, too, commends the fruits of the Spirit to us. Because like always begets like, the readings tie karma and grace to the fruits of the Spirit:

> As ye seek Him, so does like beget like. For, ye are co-laborers with Him, if ye have put on the whole of His love in thine own life.
> Feed, then, upon the fruits of the spirit. Love, hope, joy, mercy, long-suffering, brotherly love, and the contact, the growth, will be seen; and within the consciousness of the soul will the awareness come of the personality of the God in thee!   254-68

There is always cause and effect; we always reap what we sow. As we harness the power of our minds and wills and consciously choose to seek our Creator, we are healing bad karma and building good karma. Specifically, we can heal a challenge, temptation, or difficulty by choosing to respond by applying the fruits of the Spirit rather than by continuing to react from our old, unthinking habit patterns.

In poetic language, this reading compares our souls to pearls. Although we may not realize it, the irritations of life polish our souls and help them grow in beauty.

A pearl is an adornment, a thing of beauty, created through the irritation . . . which manifests itself in a lowly way to those that consider themselves of high estate; but by the very act of irritation to its own vibration is the higher vibration created, or brings about the pearl of great price . . .

Through such irritation, though, oft does the soul grow, even as the pearl . . .

This growth may not be felt in the consciousness of materialization. It is experienced by the consciousness of the soul . . .

254-68

Recognizing Grace

If ye live by grace, ye must practice grace—and be gracious.
2981-1

Sometimes we only recognize the grace of God in hindsight—after we have moved beyond some traumatic and painful event and had some time to heal. Often, with the passage of time, we begin to see that our difficulty could have been far worse. We may come to understand that this event was truly a great teacher and that we are wiser for the experience. We may even grow to realize that this challenge was for our greater good.

Like most people, I've had a number of these course corrections in my life. At the time, I thought that each disaster which befell me was the end of the world. In time, I came to know that not only was it not the end of the world, it was the beginning of new and greater opportunities and understandings. This is what the readings call turning our stumbling blocks into stepping stones. This is part of our journey to transform karma into grace.

The Eyes Have It

An eye for an eye only ends up making the whole world blind.
—Gandhi

People sometimes ask me if I am depressed about having two progressive, crippling illnesses. I tell them honestly that I'm really not. There are probably a variety of reasons for my healthy attitude, but I credit most of it to Cayce. I'm grateful that my physical challenges are chronic and not acute, that is, they are not life–threatening and will not kill me. I've had the luxury of time to experiment with them, mainly using suggestions from the readings, from which I've received most of my help. I'm also grateful that my illnesses are not very painful. I used to get killer cramps in my calf muscles, but a Cayce compound called Calcios banished them. Calcios is a paste made from bone meal that is rich in calcium and trace minerals. Being a paste, it is more quickly and completely absorbed by the body than a pill.

However, we all know that life is a series of challenges. There is something that I find more frightening than being crippled, and that is being blind. I had a brush with blindness a few years ago. Over a period of about four years, I had eight retina tears. I was very lucky. The retinas never detached, and each time, they were repaired successfully with laser surgery. Thankfully, I never had to have traditional surgery, in which my eyeball would actually have to be cut open. For all practical purposes, I've not even lost any vision except for a little ability to see my nose! And I really don't spend much time looking at my nose.

But at some point during this scary period of my life, a thought hit me hard. I asked my retina specialist, "If I lived in another time or place, I'd have been blind wouldn't I?" He nodded and said softly, "Yes." I realized then that laser surgery, which I always dreaded, had been another form of grace in my life. My good–karma mother always told me to count my blessings. Cayce certainly supports this and it doubtlessly helps to fuel my positive mental attitude.

Employment Challenges

We grow in grace, in knowledge, in understanding. **349-12**

Grace comes in many forms and disguises. Sometimes, when we are in a very low place in our lives, grace can be very hard to discern. Job karma is very common in our materialistic culture. Many people grow up believing that their job is their security. It is who they are. It is the key to a successful and prosperous life. We are taught that we must climb to the top of our profession, that we must compete and get ahead of other people, often at any cost.

I always knew I wanted to be a teacher. Yet I only spent a few years teaching in a classroom. When I tried to reenter the teaching field, after my second marital debacle, I was stunned to find that there were no jobs available in my field. After many months of terrible, temporary jobs, I took a typing course to qualify for a government job. With my limited dexterity, I only passed the typing test on the last day of the class and with a minimal score. I would never have believed that God's grace was hiding in this humiliating situation.

Although I was grateful for the federal security and benefits, not to mention the paycheck, it took many years for me to realize how hard teaching would have been on me physically as I aged and my physical challenges increased. In addition, I was able to take an early retirement from the government, whereas I would have had to work many additional years to retire from teaching. I treasure my world travels and would not have been able to take nearly as many trips if I had remained in teaching. I certainly would not have been able to write this book if I were still working. In summary, I now recognize that my not returning to the classroom was grace, and I'm clear that Someone a lot smarter than I am was looking out for me.

To Bee or Not to Bee

Do not obtain that which ye cannot make constructive in thine own experience and in the experience of those whom ye contact day by day.   5753-2

Karen Richards, a dear friend and A.R.E. member who is part of my Virginia Beach family, shared this story of how healing grace came to her in the form of a bee.

Karen had always been afraid of bees. No one wants to be stung, but she had an inner fear—an uncontrollable panic, an abject terror, that would cause her breathing to become labored, make her insides churn, and cause her to run away screaming. It wasn't just the sight of a bee—any type of buzzing near her ear would set her heart pounding. Even as she worked to control this panic and terror as she got older, she would still flinch and move quickly away from bees. This, of course, can startle them and cause the very thing she feared—being stung.

Karen had assumed that this fear had developed because she had been stung when she was about a year old. Yet she continued to wonder if this were really the reason that she was so terrified of bees and of buzzing, since she had never been stung again. As she began to walk her spiritual path and gained an understanding of past lives and karma, she had the sense, in the back of her mind, that there was more to this than a simple bee sting. Little did she know that the answer was closer to the surface than she ever imagined.

It happened in 1981. She was visiting a friend, "Mary," whom she had known in college. Mary and her husband lived in an older apartment with no air conditioning in Silver Spring, Maryland. The kitchen appliances were old and white, from the early 1960s. When Mary went into the kitchen, she discovered that a large wasp had taken up residence behind her refrigerator. Karen reports that she was ready to bolt but remembered that Mary was very allergic to bee stings. There was no bug spray in the house, and they talked about knocking on some apartment doors to borrow some or going to the grocery store to buy some. But they got some hair spray, which they hoped would kill the bee by coating its body. As Mary ventured into the kitchen, she told Karen that if she was stung, there would be only a few minutes to get her to a hospital! Karen thought to herself, "This is ridiculous. She could die from a sting and I'm just afraid." So Karen took the hair spray and had Mary wait in the living room.

As Karen began spraying in the crack between the refrigerator and the cabinets, the buzzing became loud and grew in intensity, as if the wasp was trying to fly from its hiding place. As that sound intensified, the light in the room took on an extreme brilliance and she doesn't recall seeing the stove, refrigerator, sink, or cabinets. All she could see was white and a blackness rising toward her. She let out a bloodcurdling scream and ran from the kitchen. Mary was sitting on the sofa, and her face was white with fear as she asked if Karen had been stung. Karen just sat in the living room shaking, with sweat pouring off of her. Karen told her what happened and thought that the wasp had flown toward her. Mary decided to wait until her husband came home that evening to take care of the creature, and they both went out for some well-deserved ice cream. They were both baffled by the experience, and Karen just tucked it away for a later review.

Some weeks later, when Karen was discussing metaphysics with a work colleague, she related the bee story. Her colleague suggested that she might have been reexperiencing a death from a past life, especially given the imagery of blackness rushing toward her and the buzzing. This struck a deep inner chord within Karen. Perhaps the blackness was the ground rushing up, and the buzzing was the sound of plane engines. Perhaps this was from one of the world wars. It all made sense and Karen realized that she had experienced a "breakthrough" into a past life and that the buzzing triggered the recall.

While she hasn't had a complete past–life recall, Karen has worked hard to make peace with bees. Within a year of this revelation, some bees joined Karen on a park bench and wanted to share her soda. She was able to watch them in relative calm. She talked to them, and after discovering that it was just a diet soda, the bees flew away. Karen was proud that she hadn't screamed or run but had worked to stay calm. Now she understood that it wasn't the bee sting so much but the buzzing sound that was triggering her terrifying, visceral feelings. And this she could control.

Twenty–five years later, Karen still startles when she hears a buzzing in her ears, even if it is a fly or a mosquito. Knowing what is going on enables her to control her reaction. She continues to talk to the bees and move out of their way. She really worked to control her automatic responses when her son was born, because she didn't want to translate her fears to him.

In some Native American traditions, the bee symbolizes the warrior. When a bee "drops its robe," or dies, it is powerful medicine. Karen is beginning to understand that warrior power as it crosses the dimensions of time, space, and reality.

King David
It is never too late to mend thy ways.   **5284-1**

In the following reading, Cayce uses King David as a classic example of karma and grace:

> Using the experience of David the king as an example, what was it in his experience that caused him to be called a man after God's own heart? That he did not falter, that he did not do this or that

or be guilty of every immoral experience in the category of man's relationship? Rather was it that he was sorry, and not guilty of the same offence twice!

Well that ye pattern thy study of thyself after such a life!

There may be an excuse—yes, there may be a forgiveness for those that err once; is there for twice, is there for thrice? Yea...ye [must] forgive, if ye would be forgiven! For that is the law.

5753-2

David's story should give us all heart. He made many serious mistakes, but he sincerely repented and did not repeat them. Since we all err many times, forgiveness is key if we seek to move from karma to grace. The law of cause and effect is always operative. As we apply the fruits of the Spirit and forgive others their transgressions, ours are also forgiven.

11

The Most Important Thing You Can Do–Know Your Spiritual Ideal

For there is only one ideal in **human** *relationships . . . "Love thy neighbor as thyself."*   **1598-1**

Edgar Cayce, the "Sleeping Prophet," addressed the following strong statement about the importance of ideals to each and every person: "[T]he most important experience of this or any individual entity is to first know what is the ideal—spiritually." (357-13) But after reading this, most of us probably wonder, What does that really mean? How do we go about knowing our spiritual ideal, and what do we do after that? Let's examine this important advice from some different angles.

To begin very simply, the dictionary defines an ideal as a standard of perfection, beauty, or excellence; a model for imitation; an ultimate aim or endeavor.[1] We all have ideals, whether we recognize them or not. We may call them by other names, such as wishes, dreams, or goals. They motivate many of our actions. They frequently guide our decision–making. They fill our conversations and our daydreams. For example, we all want a happy, healthy, successful life, however we define it. We want loving, fulfilling relationships, whatever that may mean to us. We want jobs that pay well but that also satisfy us and make a contribution to society if possible. We may want to live in certain kinds of homes, have a certain appearance or status, participate in certain activities, belong to certain organizations, and so on. The list goes on and on. Cayce tells us that it is crucial to our very soul development to wake up and take charge of our ideals and decide if they are indeed what we want to literally build into the fabric of our lives—both present and future.

> ... that which the self sets as its ideal—whether pertaining to the material, the mental or the spiritual forces—should be the guide, should be the measuring stick always for decisions that the entity may make in associations or in activities; whether these deal with spiritual forces or the mental or material activities.
>
> And unless one does hold or set an ideal, one continues to be a drifter; and never is at peace with self.   1538-1

In 1932 a twenty-year-old man asked Cayce for spiritual advice to guide him through college. Cayce told him: "*Know* the ideal. Measure the moral life, the social life, the material life, the spiritual life, by that standard. Lose not sight of that thou believest." (488-6)

The same year, a thirty-five-year-old man courageously asked the entranced Cayce, "Am I too selfish?" Cayce's guidance went straight to our subject of ideals.

> Selfishness is the greater fault in *most* individuals. There should be set before self an ideal, a *spiritual* ideal. Not such an ideal that "I would like to have a house like John Smith's, and a wife that dresses like Mrs. Smith, and a car like John Smith's boy runs, or a dog or a horse such as those." *That's* material! Rather set an ideal in the *spiritual* sense, and know that he that would be greatest among men will be the servant of all.   912-1

Thus ideals can tell us how we are doing at all levels—spiritually, mentally, and physically—in our lives right now. Working consciously and consistently with them helps us move into closer harmony with our true spiritual natures. Using ideals helps us close the gap between our theory and our practice. The readings provide a great deal of valuable guidance about how to thoughtfully and purposefully choose and set ideals. Cayce frequently stresses the seriousness of this effort.

> One of the influences that must first be builded, then, is to first know thy ideals—spiritually, mentally, materially. And in the spiritual, know that the ideal must be that which is able to keep whatever may be committed unto it against *any* experience. In the mental, it must be ever constructive, creative in its influence, in its activity. In the material it must be not what you would want others to do for you, but the ideal manner and way in which ye must meet . . . thy fellow man.
>
> These . . . should be studied, analyzed, thought through; and, no matter *what* the cost may be, they should be lived up to . . .
>
> . . . it will bring harmony, contentment, and sufficient of *every* worldly, spiritual, material thing necessary for thy soul development.
>
> Then, what thy destiny is depends upon what ye will do with thyself in relationship to thy ideal.   2021-1

Notice that ideals are so important that Cayce uses the word *first* twice in the first sentence. Clearly, ideals are something that we should establish sooner rather than later. Once set, the spiritual ideal should be adhered to "against *any* experience"—a very high bar indeed. The reading instructs that the mental ideal should be constructive; it should promote self-improvement and development. It should also be creative—inventive, productive, and imaginative. The material ideal should not focus on what we want to get from other people but on how we treat them; for both the Bible and Cayce tell us that how we treat others is how we are treating God. Now that is a very sobering thought. Stop and think about it. How did we treat God today through our interactions with other people? And last but not least, each of us should thoroughly analyze our ideals, and "no matter *what* the cost may be, they should be lived up to"—yet another very high bar.

To be sure, setting ideals is very serious spiritual business. It is using our God-given free will to choose whom we will serve—God or ourselves. But the promise of this effort is very great—"it will bring harmony, contentment, and sufficient of *every* worldly, spiritual, material thing necessary for thy soul development." Everything necessary for our soul development—that is what we are here for, why we incarnated, our very purpose. What more could we possibly want? How can we not seize this opportunity right now to begin to do what each of us came here to do? We can control our very destiny by faithfully and sincerely seeking to live up to our ideals.

How to Set Ideals

. . . the purposes of the entrance of an entity into a material plane
. . . to choose that which is its ideal.   **987-4**

The following reading tells us in a simple and straightforward fashion how to go about the process of setting ideals. Get some paper and a pencil, and try doing this along with Cayce right now. The reading said to use a pencil because we would be erasing frequently as we grow through working with this process, so don't worry about making a mistake. If you're making a sincere effort, there are no mistakes: "For, God looketh and judgeth not as man. Man seeth the outward appearance; God looketh on and knoweth the heart!" (294-198)

> In choosing and in analyzing self and the ideal, do not merely carry these in mind but put them . . . upon the paper . . . Write *Physical*. Draw a line, write *Mental*. Draw a line, write *Spiritual*.
>
> Put under each, beginning with the spiritual, (for all that is in mind must first come from a spiritual concept) what is thy spiritual concept of the ideal, whether it be Jesus, Buddha, mind, material, God or whatever is the word which indicates to self the ideals spiritual.
>
> Then under the *mental* heading write the ideal mental attitude, as may arise from concepts of the spiritual, in relationship to self, to home, to friends, to neighbors, to thy enemies, to things, to conditions.
>
> Then write . . . the ideal material . . . what has brought, what does bring into [physical] manifestation the spiritual and mental ideals. What relationships does such bring to things, to individuals, to situations?   **5091-3**

In 1926 Cayce gave a rabbi's wife this profound advice about ideals:

> ... for there is *one* ideal ... to make the Creative Energy ... called by many names ... the ideal, and to make the mind, the body mind, the heart mind, the active force in the life for *others* and for self, for the greater service to that Energy, or to God, is *service* to the fellow man ...
>
> It is not that the entity should make self popular with the people—rather make self popular with God, through service to God's children, or to the men whom [the] entity would serve.
>
> 4159-1

Like so much spiritual work, setting and applying ideals is paradoxically both very easy and challenging. Choosing and writing our ideals on a sheet of paper is just the first step. But to seriously engage in this process of holding to our ideals "against *any* experience ... no matter *what* the cost" and refining them as we grow through applying them is where the real work and rewards will occur. As the readings so often tell us, all we have to do is make a start. We learn by doing. Simply begin. Keep the paper with your ideals on it where you will see it frequently, and use your ideals faithfully in your interactions with others. It will be well worth the effort. Your soul will smile.

Living Our Ideals

> ... *what one believes alone is not sufficient; but what one does about that one believes either makes for advancement or growth, or retardment.* 262-55

Now it's time to try living what you've written on your paper. "For, it is not merely what one believes that counts, but what one does *about* that believed!" (2405-1) No one limits us but us: "As to the abilities of the entity, then, these are only limited by the application of the self to its ideal." (3189-2)

What, then, is this as an ideal?

As concerning thy fellow man, He gave, "As ye would that
others do to you, do ye even so to them," . . .

This, then, is that attitude of mind that puts away hates,
malice, anxiety, jealousy. And it creates in their stead, in that
Mind is the Builder, the fruits of the spirit—love, patience,
mercy, longsuffering, kindness, gentleness . . . They break down
barriers, they bring peace and harmony, they bring the outlook
upon life of not finding fault because someone "forgot," someone's
judgment was bad, someone was selfish today. These ye can
overlook, for so did He.   357-13

Ever wonder why the world sometimes seems to be in such a mess?
Collectively, we are the world. It's all about how we treat each other. If
we want to move forward, Cayce tells us to apply our ideals and bring
help and hope to someone today.

It is necessary, to be sure, that there be a coordinating of the ideals
and ideal relationships with those whom the body may contact
day by day. But to let little differences, little animosities, little
hurts, interfere with the real ideal and purpose of an entity or soul
is to go backward—rather than onward with . . . that which will
be helpful and hopeful . . .   815-3

Cayce's readings also tell us that we sometimes rationalize our choices
by using emergencies or other life situations as excuses to indulge our
physical desires instead of applying our ideals. Our higher and lower
selves are at war within us. A simple example that I have been known
to use is— "I'm tired; I worked hard today; I deserve a dish of ice cream
before I go to bed." Then I'm unhappy when I gain weight! I guess I
could call it the ice cream war.

The mind uses its spiritual ideals to build upon. And the mind
also uses the material desires as the destructive channels, or it is
the interference by the material desires that prevents a body and
a mind from keeping in perfect accord with its ideal.

Thus, these continue ever in the material plane to be as

warriors one with another. Physical emergencies or physical conditions may oft be used as excuses, or as justifications for the body choosing to do this or that.   357-13

And, finally, remember this admonition: "Then, knowing the ideal, practice it. Don't have an ideal and then not practice it in thy daily activities." (5256-1) Once you've set ideals, use them. Don't ever set them aside. Give yourself a chance to know that deep, inner, soul-level joy that heading in the right direction can bring you.

12

A Closer Look at Free Will– God's Greatest Gift

*The will is the birthright of the Creator to each soul, that it may
choose for itself that direction it—the entity, the soul—may take.*

2170-1

Free will or predestination—are we really free to make our own choices,
or are we victims of fate? This is truly one of the greatest philosophical
questions of all times and has been debated for centuries. Edgar Cayce's
source answered this and other age-old questions with amazing clarity
in reading 5749-14, which was given to Tom Sugrue, Edgar's first biog-
rapher, as he was writing the philosophy chapter for *There Is a River*. Since
free will is so central to who we really are, how we got to where we are
today, and what we can do about it, let's look at a portion of this very
profound reading.

The Origin of Free Will

There is set before thee life and death, good and evil. Choose thou!

333-6

Sugrue asked Cayce to start at the very beginning, with the creation
of our souls. Quickly one of the greatest yet most fundamental premises

of this philosophy emerged. It concerned our essence; Cayce's source spoke about who we really are.

> (Q) Should [the reason for creation] be given as God's desire to experience Himself, God's desire for companionship, God's desire for expression, or in some other way?
>
> (A) God's desire for companionship and expression.
>
> (Q) [Regarding] that which is variously called evil, darkness, negation, sin. Should it be said that this condition existed as a necessary element of creation, and the soul, given free will, found itself with the power to indulge in it, or lose itself in it? Or should it be said that this is a condition created by the activity of the soul itself? Should it be described, in either case, as a state of consciousness, a gradual lack of awareness of self and self's relation to God?
>
> (A) It is the free will and its losing itself in its relationship to God.
>
> (Q) Should [the fall of man] be described as something which was inevitable in the destiny of souls, or something which God did not desire, but which He did not prevent once He had given free will? The problem here is to reconcile the omniscience of God and His knowledge of all things with the free will of the soul and the soul's fall from grace.
>
> (A) He did not prevent, once having given free will . . . [T]he beginnings of sin . . . were in [souls] seeking expression of themselves outside of [God's] plan . . . Thus it was the individual, see?
>
> Having given free will, then—though having the foreknowledge, though being omnipotent and omnipresent—it is only when the soul . . . *chooses* that God knows the end thereof.
>
> 5749-14

Three Key Concepts

. . . the will is an attribute of the soul, and the whole development of an entity.   **274-1**

Three key concepts related to free will emerge from this incredible reading. Let's explore and clarify each of these concepts further as well as examine some other relevant readings.

1. God created us out of a desire for companionship and expression.

> *... losing that companionship [with God] by choice of that which*
> *would satisfy or gratify a material desire only.*   3645-1

That we were created to be companions of God is an awesome thought filled with unimaginable potential. God is inherently creative, and we are a part of the results! We, too, are inherently creative and are called to use our gifts responsibly. Our karmic struggles in the flesh serve a high purpose, to purify us that we may regain our original oneness with our Creator.

> ... we were made for the purpose of being companions with Him, a little lower than the angels who behold His face ever yet as heirs, as joint heirs with Him who *is* the Savior, the Way ...
> 1567-2

> ... souls were made to be companions with the Creator. And through error, through rebellion, through contempt, through hatred, through strife, it became necessary then that all pass under the rod; tempted in the fires of flesh; purified, that they may be fit companions for the *glory* that may be thine.   262-89

> ... the soul of man, thy soul, encompasses *all* in this solar system or in others.
> For, we are joint heirs with that universal force we call God — if we seek to do His biddings. If our purposes are not in keeping with that Creative Force, or God, then we may be a hindrance. And ... it has not appeared nor even entered into the heart of man to know the glories the Father has prepared for those that love Him.   5755-2

2. Evil is the result of our free will and losing our relationship to God.

> *... man, in his headstrongness, harkens oft to that which would*

separate him from his Maker!   **262-56**

The Cayce readings lay the answer to another great philosophical question, the nature and cause of evil, squarely on the altar of our free will. Evil is the result of our poor choices, our misuse of our God–given free will. While still in spirit, we squandered our oneness with God and forgot who we were.

> . . . all souls in the beginning were one with the Father. The separation, or turning away, brought evil. Then there became the necessity of the awareness of self's being out of accord with, or out of the realm of blessedness . . .   262-56

> For man is the co-creator with the builder and the maker of the universe, and yet creates conditions, positions, thoughts, that often turn and rend his own self.   3351-1

When Cayce was asked what had separated spirit from its source, "or what causes good and evil," he replied forcefully, "Desire! *Desire!*" (5752–3) Each of us here on Earth in flesh bodies lets desire overrule our God–given free will.

3. God gave us completely free will. He does not interfere in our choices or prevent our mistakes.

Man alone is given that birthright of free will. He alone may defy his God!   5757-1

From the beginning, when we were created as souls, God allowed us total and complete freedom to make our own choices. He still does, despite the consequences. That is how we learn. Cayce explains that God does not want us to be robots. He wants us to choose, wants us to want, wants us to be with Him—one with Him.

> But the *will* is of self, else ye would not indeed be the child of the Creative and Living Force or God that ye are; but as an automaton.   1538-1

> God does not even answer for you. He gives you the free will to

use as ye *will*. For He does not want, does not have, other than that one choosing to be equal with Him. If He had to knock you in the head to do it, or you had to become an automaton and pushed about, could you be equal with the Creative Forces? Answer within yourself!   2981-4

God knew that only those who purposefully chose oneness with Him over all else would be worthy companions. Thus, when gifting us with free will in the beginning, He created levels of awareness and opportunities that would truly challenge our freedom and hone our power of choice.

The Creator, in seeking to . . . create a being worthy of companionship, realized that such a being would result only from a free will exercising its divine inheritance and through its own efforts find its Maker. Thus, to make the choice really a Divine one caused the existence of states of consciousness, that would indeed tax the free will of a soul . . .   262-56

So, if at times you feel taxed in responding to life's convoluted twists and turns, know that you may well be facing decisions that will influence your very soul growth and spiritual destiny. This obstacle course is designed by our Creator to challenge us and to make us worthy companions to Him.

Our freedom of choice is so total and absolute that despite being all-powerful, even God does not know our future until we choose a direction:

God Himself knows not what man will destine to do with himself, else would He have repented that He had made man? He has given man free will.   262-86

It is the use of our will, through the innumerable choices that we have made over eons, which has made us unique individuals, each soul different from every other soul. It is also our use of our free will that triggers cause and effect—our karma—which then limits our future range of choice. Because our actions always trigger reactions, we have invited circumstances into our lives that we must confront until we learn the intended lessons. We are the result of all that we have ever been and all the choices that we have ever made. The better choices we make now, the better future we create for ourselves and others.

Thus we find that one of the greatest lessons in life is that free will and karma go hand in hand. God knew that with souls who have both the vast power of mind to build and create and also totally free, unfettered will, problems could well occur. Indeed, even chaos was possible. So, although it may not seem like it, karma is also a gift from God. It is cosmic feedback. It is how we learn. God created a lawful universe. As we have seen, Cayce stated many, many times, that it is natural law: "Like begets like." (254–73) So what we do with our free will always comes back to us, for good or ill, even if it is delayed. It is always up to us. Thus it is God's plan that no matter how long it takes, we will learn to make choices in harmony with the Higher will and claim our spiritual heritage.

Right use of our free will is the key to reclaiming our divine heritage. It's the only way we can mature and develop to our spiritual potential. Near the end of this philosophy reading given for Tom Sugrue, Cayce not only reiterated the primacy of our free will, he made an astounding promise: No matter how far we have fallen, through our use of will we may know God.

> (Q) Are hereditary, environment and will equal factors in aiding or retarding the entity's development?
> (A) Will is the greater factor, for it may overcome any or all of the others; provided that will is made one with the pattern, see? For, no influence of heredity, environment or what not, surpasses the will; else why would there have been that pattern shown in which the individual soul, no matter how far astray it may have gone, may enter with Him into the holy of holies?   5749-14

The central point of the story of mankind in the Earth is that we must all remember our ultimate spiritual destiny. And the key to getting there is to discipline our free will.

... the spirit is the spark, or portion of the Divine that is in every entity, whether complete or [evolving] to that completeness ...

All souls were created in the beginning, and are finding their way back to whence they came ...

Where does the soul go when fully developed? To its Maker.

3744-5

... the will must be the ever guiding factor to lead man on, ever upward.   3744-4

Making Business Decisions

... for will is the factor in the mind of man that must be exercised.
3744-4

The life readings are full of people, often in pain and confusion, asking questions and seeking guidance from Edgar Cayce. Many, many times he tossed the ball right back to the questioner by quoting one of his favorite biblical injunctions about making choices: "choose you this day whom ye will serve" (Joshua 24:15) or "I have set before thee this day life and good, death and evil ... choose ... " (Deuteronomy 30:15, 19)

Many of Edgar Cayce's supporters were businessmen, like Mr. [419], who asked questions about their careers. We can see in this response from Cayce that the Source could be stern.

... first there must be a determination within self as to what *is* to be the activities; whether sweeping streets, running engines, motors, flying machines, digging ditches, or what! But *choose!* and then stick to that! It's the only way that those abilities that are latent may be developed in *any* entity; anyone that will build is to apply self *in* the field, *in* the way, *in* that which is *chosen* as the life's work! ... *whatever* is chosen, do *that!*   419-3

This advice applies to us all. This reading tells us that the only way any of us can develop abilities that lie sleeping within us is to make a choice and stick to it. The law of cause and effect will give us feedback, and we will continue to learn and grow as we move ahead, step by step, and make our own choices. Cayce told another indecisive businessman to make his own decisions.

> If this is the desire, if this is what is wished, then pull up stakes and do it! This *must* be *determined* by *self!* It will *not* be given from here that you should hang *any* hope on *any* tree, on *any* place, on *any* thing, save on God—and let Him meet thee in self! as to *what* is the choice to be made, *ever*, by Self.   333-6

Making Romantic Decisions

Marry the one the body loves, regardless of profession or business!
4586-4

Other seekers came to Cayce with questions of the heart. Again, his advice was that they needed to make their own decisions.

> (Q) When should this body marry?
> (A) When it gets ready to!
> (Q) Has she met the proper man?
> (A) If she thinks so, yes! . . .
> (Q) Should the body marry a business or professional man?
> (A) Marry the one the body loves, *regardless* of profession or business!   4586-4

A 29-year-old woman asked Cayce:

> (Q) What will be the effect on my life of this marriage to [. . .]?
> (A) What wilt thou *allow* it to become? This depends . . . upon the choices . . .
>
> Man and woman are free-willed. What will ye *make of* such an association?
>
> If ye choose the right—contentment, happiness and joy.
>
> If it is for self and the glorification and magnification of self—inharmony, distrust, turmoils and strife.
>
> The law is before thee—and it is *sure!*   1470-2

Don't Listen To Others

... not through counsel or advice from any source outside self,
save the higher spiritual source.   *349-14*

Often in seeking to be helpful, we assume that we know what is best
for someone else and offer our advice. Just as God allows us totally free
choice, we must respect the rights of others to make their own choices,
even if we think that they are making a mistake. This forty–eight–year–
old woman was told very bluntly in her reading that she had a problem:

> ... you listen to others too much! ...
> Know that thy body, thy mind, thy soul, is a manifestation of
> God in the earth—as is every other soul; and that thy body is
> indeed the temple of the living God. All the good, then, all the
> God, then, that ye may know, is manifested in and through
> thyself—and not what somebody else thinks, not what somebody
> else does!   2970-1

This reading hits the heart of the issue. We are each a manifestation
of God; our bodies are temples of God; all the good, or God, that we
may know comes from within us, not from other people. Many times
Cayce repeated this kind of guidance. Listening to others creates confusion. We must make our decisions based on our spiritual ideals. If we
will trust, God will help us even with the smallest matter.

> These should be the answers ever. That choices are made by
> counsel here or counsel there only makes for confusion within
> self, oft. Rather meet within thine own self thy Maker, and let the
> guide come *there* as to what ye shall do.   333-6

> And, irrespective of what has been said by others, or associations
> or connections with same, the decision should be ruled, regu-
> lated, by that [which] self holds as the ideal; or the spiritual
> influence that impels the activity.   349-14

> For, would that all souls could know that He, the Giver of good
> and perfect gifts, is ever ready and willing to assist, even in the

minutest details of a human experience, or in those things that deal with the activities of a soul with its fellow man, if the trust will but be put in Him . . .   590-1

How to Make Good Decisions

Do not too oft accept what others say, unless *it answers to a some-*
thing deep within self.   3051-2

Thankfully, Cayce's source gave us some excellent guidance on how to make good decisions.

(Q) What will help me most in coming to right decisions as to my life?
(A) Prayer and meditation, to be sure . . .

Then, in thine own mind, decide as to whether this or that direction is right. Then pray on it, and leave it alone. Then suddenly ye will have the answer, yes or no.

Then, with that yes or no, take it again to Him in prayer, "Show me the way." And yes or no will again direct thee from deep within.

That is practical direction.   3250-1

(Q) How can one be sure that a decision is in accordance with God's will?
(A) Ask . . . the . . . conscious self, "Shall I do this or not?" The voice will answer within. Then meditate, ask the same, yes or no. You may be very sure if thine own conscious self and the divine self is in accord, you are truly in that activity indicated, "My spirit beareth witness with thy spirit." You can't get far wrong in following the word, as ye call the word of God.

2072-14

Obviously, Mrs. [3250] didn't catch the spirit of Cayce's advice when she asked, "Is it true, as I have felt, that I have enemies—those who are trying to do me out of my inheritance?" Cayce chided her:

Ye have no enemies. Let this ever be within thine own heart: Do *right* in self. And that which is thine own cannot, will not be taken from thee. Those who try such are enemies to themselves. Look not upon them as enemies to thee. Feel sorry for them for their misconstruction of right.   3250-1

The bottom line from Cayce places the ultimate responsibility squarely on us: "Know deep within self that nothing may separate thee from the knowledge or the love of God save thy own self." (2990-2) Making choices has very serious karmic consequences. Free will is our pathway to companionship with God.

13

Application–the Final Step

Do not attempt to be good but rather good for something! 830-3

Ever ask yourself, when you're so busy you don't know what to do next, What in life is truly worth doing? Here is how Edgar Cayce answers that question. "Only that which produces . . . experiences that may make a citizen a better citizen, a father a better father, a mother a better mother, a neighbor a better neighbor, is constructive." (5753-2) In light of that guidance, we should all probably drop a number of things we do and reshuffle our priorities.

In terms of learning about our past lives, that same reading continues:

> . . . to find that ye only lived, died and were buried under the cherry tree in Grandmother's garden does not make thee one whit better neighbor, citizen, mother or father!
>
> But to know that ye spoke unkindly and suffered for it, and in the present may correct it by being righteous—*that* is worth while!   5753-2

What this reading is saying is that all our activities, including insights about our past lives, should be used constructively to promote personal growth.

The readings consistently emphasize that it is through applying what we know in the present that we learn and grow, which is what we are here to do. And that is precisely how we transform our karma into grace and move from painful challenges to inner peace. This chapter will highlight some key concepts from Cayce that, when applied, invite grace into our lives.

First Things First—Deepen Your Relationship With God

But seek ye first the kingdom of God . . . Matthew 6:33

Psychologists and counselors are always telling us to improve our communication with others. Who could be more important to communicate with than our Creator? The first and by far the most important step to take if you'd like to experience the spiritual alchemy of transforming karma into grace is to simply talk to God. Get to know your Creator. Cayce put it this way: "seeking Him first is the whole duty of an entity." (2549-1) Nothing could be easier, because of who we really are in our innermost beings. You must be on speaking terms with God, unless you have no interest in growing but are satisfied to simply drift along with life's currents. If you're already friends with God, that relationship can and should be deepened. The potential is literally unlimited, as is shown in this amazing statement from Cayce.

(Q) What is the highest possible psychic realization—etc?
(A) That God, the Father, speaks directly to the sons of men— even as He has promised.   440-4

Cayce clarified the nature of our communication with God this way to a young seeker in 1932.

(Q) What change has come into my spiritual life or character?
(A) This . . . is ready for an awakening. Seek, then, to know self,

> to know self's relationships to the Creative Forces that may be
> *manifest* in the activities of the mental and the spiritual life!
> *Know* that the Creative Energy called God may be as personal as
> an individual will allow same to be; for the Spirit is in the image
> of the Creative Forces and seeks manifestation. It may take that
> personality, that will be allowed by the individual itself; for we are
> co-laborers, co-creators with that Energy we call God, that
> Energy we call Universal Forces.   391-4

Cayce's source tells us that even the nature of our relationship with God is up to us and our all-powerful free will. That holy relationship can be just as up close and personal or just as impersonal and distant as we desire it to be. All we have to do is invite it into our lives. Our power is unlimited because, in the beautiful language of the readings, we are co-creators with the Highest.

In 1935 Cayce advised a young man to "take the *Lord* in partnership with thee! But be honest with *Him* and with thyself, as you would have *Him* to be honest and sincere with thee!" (815-3)

At this point in my life, I talk to God like a dear friend many times each day. I both thank Him for His bounty in my life and ask for His help and guidance with my concerns. My access to God is immediate. I don't need a password. I never get a busy signal. I don't have to make an appointment. He doesn't judge or criticize me but calms and comforts me. Seeing how this process has continued to enrich my life and yield inner peace continues to strengthen my faith. Personally, this inner dialogue has been by far the most rewarding part of my spiritual journey. It has yielded rich insights and creative ideas. If you're not on speaking terms with God, it's high time to begin. Try it right now; talk to God in any manner that is comfortable for you.

> Thus, as ye apply—the answer comes . . . [In] putting away the
> worldly things ye take hold upon the spiritual things, knowing
> that the worldly are but the shadows of the real.
>
>   And thus, as ye come into the light of His countenance, it
> maketh thy heart glad in the consciousness of "*I am Thine—
> Thou art mine.*"   987-4

Let's look at prayer and meditation—two of the best ways to communicate with God. Cayce said that they are two sides of the same coin. A.R.E.'s *A Search For God* Study Group text puts it this way: "In prayer we speak to God, in meditation God speaks to us."[1]

Punctuate Each Day with Prayer

Talk with Him from thine inner self, as though He were physically present; for mentally and spiritually He is ever present.   1152-9

Through working with prayer, we use our mind, which Cayce identifies as the builder, to reprogram ourselves. As we upgrade our thoughts, we upgrade our actions. Cayce's source put it humorously: "when the entity has sung Halleluiah it was much harder to say 'dammit.'" (622-6) These efforts will move us closer to our ideals and to conscious awareness of our spiritual natures.

> Remember that He has given (and it applies to thee . . .), "Though ye wander far afield, if ye call I will hear—and answer speedily." That is the promise of thy Maker, thy God! And He answers to thee within!   1977-1

Each day is a new opportunity. Prayer should be a two-way street, not just asking for things but giving thanks. The readings stress this: "O that people would learn the true meaning of just being grateful, and saying Thank You, and meaning it!" (2778-2) As the saying goes, I try to have an attitude of gratitude. My mother always told me to count my blessings and I do. I like to start my day with thanksgiving. Whether I'm still lazing in bed or in the shower rushing to be somewhere soon, I bless my family on their way. I also keep a personal prayer list, and even if I'm in motion, I try to remember those people who have special needs. For me, the key phrase in the Lord's Prayer is "Thy will be done," so I give my day to God. I know He can see the big picture that I can't. I surround myself with the light of the Lord and seek to go forward in that spirit, that consciousness each day.

At night before I go to sleep, I think back over my day and try to evaluate how I've done that day in terms of applying my ideals. I make mental notes about where and with whom I want to do better. Last but not least, I end the day as I started it, by always giving thanks. I find that recognizing my blessings is especially helpful in keeping my emotional balance when I've had a rough day.

> As much as practical, leave off worry. Know that there is that trust, that faith, that hope in the Creative Forces—which may cast out fear. Why worry? For worry only makes matters worse. *Pray*, rather than worry. He answereth prayer. 760-3

Edgar Cayce's granddaughter, Gail Cayce Schwartzer, lives in Virginia Beach and shared this beautiful story of answered prayer.

Gail didn't marry until late in life and began trying for a pregnancy around forty. The first "tries" ended with miscarriages, and the first that seemed to work later miscarried as well. More than discouraged, she decided to check out what her grandfather gave in his readings for conceiving and maintaining a pregnancy. After a little research, Gail found the following affirmation, which had been given for an individual who was trying to get pregnant and maintain the pregnancy:

> Hold often to that which must have been the awareness of the Mother of the Master, when there was made the awareness, the quickening of the body-forces through the Spirit of God; "That my body, now, is in that position, that condition, wherein God, the Father, may make manifest in me, through me, *life*, God Himself made flesh; that I, through my body, may be aware of His presence with me, that I may give to the world a channel through which greater blessings, greater knowledge, greater love, greater hope, may be made manifest in the world." 1523-8

Gail held on to that affirmation daily and became pregnant. She continued to hold on to the affirmation daily, and coincidence or not, this pregnancy was successful—at forty-two, she had a baby boy, who is now twenty years old.

While working on this book, I had an experience of an instant answer to prayer. At a large gathering, I saw a friend from out of town whom I don't see very often. A few days later during my prayer time after meditation, I felt moved to ask silently, Lord, where did I know this person before? To my utter amazement, in a way that is very hard to describe, the answer hung in the question. It was almost like a silent echo. A one-word answer was just right there in my mind immediately after I asked the question. As I thought about the answer, which was the name of a foreign city, I knew that it made sense. Earlier in this lifetime, I had traveled in a group with this person, and she had done me a kindness in that very city! I had been feeling ill and upset and she had comforted me. So I thanked God for the insight and went on with my day.

About two weeks later, I got a strong urge to call this woman. I resisted the urge because I didn't know her very well, and I wasn't sure what to say to her about this experience. I also didn't know how she would react if I asked her about a past life. My resistance was short-lived, because the urge was insistent. So I said a little prayer and asked God that if I were really supposed to call her, she would be at home and answer the phone. Indeed, that is exactly what happened. She answered, and after a short chat, I told her of my meditation experience. She was silent for a moment and then told me, "I must be very resistant to the reincarnation hints I get in my dreams because sometimes I actually hear a short statement being read or I see the printed words myself about a particular past-life experience. Sometime ago one of the statements made was that I had lived in the South of France, where I had been a nun"! After that, we were silent for a while but appreciative of both the experiences and the confirmation.

In summary, this wonderful quote from Cayce about prayer says it all:

> ... never worry as long as you can pray. When you can't pray—
> you'd better begin to worry! For then you have something to
> worry about!   3569-1

The Magic of Meditation
... do you not know that your body is the temple of the Holy Spirit
who is in you, whom you have from God ... ? 1 Corinthians 6:19

The Cayce readings tell us dozens of times that learning meditation is essential: "For ye must learn to meditate—just as ye have learned to walk, to talk . . . " (281–41) Inside our physical body is our immortal soul. We must discover it and learn to communicate with it.

> Thy body is indeed the temple of the living God. There He hath promised to meet thee. There He does commune with those that seek within the holy of holies. 2787-1

> He has promised to meet thee within the temple of thine own body. For as has been given, thy body is the temple of the living God; a tabernacle, yea, for thy soul. And in the holy of holies within thine own consciousness He may walk and talk with thee.
> 987-4

When a music teacher asked Cayce in 1942 about meditation, the Source responded enthusiastically.

> (Q) Is it possible to meditate and obtain needed information?
> (A) On any subject! whether you are going digging for fishing worms or playing a concerto! 1861-12

I don't fish, nor do I play concertos, but I do meditate. Recently I had a very surprising experience during meditation. I had turned my ankle very severely, and it was swollen and painful. Being a Cayce person, I rubbed castor oil on it, and that seemed to help. However, one day while meditating, I saw a pair of shoes in my mind's eye. I was not asking about my ankle and certainly was not asking about shoes, but I realized this vision was a gift of guidance. I recognized the shoes as a pair of sturdy, roomy running shoes that I had bought at Wal–Mart a couple of years before but had never worn. They were buried in a closet somewhere among the array of shoes that I have for my challenged and frequently unhappy feet. I dug out the shoes and tried them on. They were perfect—very supportive and big enough to accommodate an ankle support. Like Edgar says, meditation can be very practical. The main purpose of meditation is not for problem–solving, but it is a very welcome byproduct. We meditate for attunement, and as inner communication improves, these gifts come to us.

Be a Channel of Blessings to Others

. . . our approach to the Throne of grace . . . will be leaning upon the arm of someone we have attempted, sincerely, to serve and aid.   **2733-2**

Beautifully phrased, Cayce often urges us to be channels of blessings to others in our lives. Just as meditation and prayer are two sides of the same coin, so seeking God within and service to our fellow man without are also two facets of the same pilgrimage. "Service to others is the highest service to God." (257-10) As is so often the case, Cayce's counsel is based upon biblical text: "But he who is greatest among you shall be your servant." (Matthew 23:11) Since we are all both one with our Creator and souls created in His image, what we do to others, we also do to our God as well as to ourselves!

> . . . Mind is the Builder, and ye build . . . through the application of [mind] in thy dealings with . . . thy fellow man, either that which is eternal—as good, as righteousness, as patience, as brotherly love, as kindness—or ye starve thy soul with the husks that satisfy only the desires of the body for the moment . . .
>
> And it is only the things of the spirit that are eternal, or that can bring that harmony which is so necessary in the experience of each soul as it journeys through the veil of the earth or dwells in the shadows of sorrow, or finds in the bright lights of the promises of tomorrow the glories that may come *only* from just being kind, just doing *every* day, in *every* way, just that to others ye would have others do to you.   1551-2

These are not just beautiful words. The readings teach that, given the law of cause and effect, they are literally true: "For that ye give of yourself in service to others, that ye retain. These come back to self—as in the sowing of good deeds." (1319-2) This reading reminds us of both the law of karma and the powerful reality of our thoughts about other people.

Speaking negatively or even thinking ill of others will return to us in kind.

> Learn the lesson well of the spiritual truth: Criticize not unless ye wish to be criticized. For, with what measure ye mete it is measured to thee again. It may not be in the same way, but ye cannot even *think* bad of another without it affecting thee in a . . . destructive nature. Think *well* of others, and if ye cannot speak well of them don't speak! but don't think it either!   2936-2

> . . . every thought is as a deed, and . . . may be made a miracle or a crime.   996-11

Not only are we told to refrain from negativity in our relationships, Cayce urges us to be actively kind and positive. My simple standard when making a difficult decision is to consider whether or not what I'm about to do is loving. Given the scope of our past experiences, we cannot know what circumstances others may face.

> Speak gently, speak kindly to those who falter. Ye know not *their* own temptation, nor the littleness of their understanding. Judge not as to this or that activity of another; rather pray that the light may shine even in *their* lives as it *has* in thine.   2112-1

> (Q) How can I use my abilities at the present time to best serve humanity?
> (A) By filling to the best possible purpose *and* ability that place, that niche the body, mind *and* soul occupies; being the *best* husband, the best neighbor, the *best* friend to each and every individual the body meets; for would one fail in meeting those obligations that one takes, they become worse *than* the infidel . . . but he that . . . is willing to become as naught that they may *serve* the better in *whatever* capacity as a merchant, be the best merchant; as a neighbor, the *best* neighbor; as a friend, the *best* friend.   99-8

Cayce summed up human relationships this way: " . . . there is so much good in the worst of us, and so much bad in the best of us, it does not behoove that *any* of us should find the fault one with another!" (1158–15)

Touched by a Teapot

I want to share a personal story of how past–life clues led me to healing some karma. Past–life clues are all around us. We just don't see them unless we really look. One day, when I had to move some breakables because I was having a new stove delivered, it hit me for the first time that I had two statues of Buddha in my living room and a third in my study. I later realized that I had another one in the bedroom. Of course, I knew that I'd been Buddhist in a past life, probably more than once. I had bought the white porcelain Buddha when I was nineteen years old and still kept it in a prominent place on an antique shelf, which resembled an altar, in my study. How many Americans have four Buddhas in their homes?

As soon as the new stove was installed, I drove out of state to help my late mother's best friend through some surgery. I grew up with Aunt Fay's family, and although she is not an aunt of my blood, she has always been an aunt of my heart. I had never been in her new house, and when I arrived, I was immediately struck by the fact that her house was full of blue and white Chinese porcelain. I, too, like that porcelain and have several pieces in my house. In fact, I had dragged a heavy, antique, blue and white porcelain cricket box back from a trip to China. My mother, who dealt in antiques, said that I should have bought several of them. As Aunt Fay and I talked about this, she pointed out that she also had three Buddhas in her living room!

I thought that this blue and white porcelain had been popular in China during the Ming Dynasty, around 1350 to 1600 AD. It wasn't a great leap to recognize that this woman, with whom I'd always felt a close bond, and I had shared a past life in Ming China, probably with my mother. (Interestingly, Mom never wanted to visit China, although her home contained many oriental antiques.) When I asked Aunt Fay how she felt about going to China, she replied that it made her fearful to even think about it. In contrast, I absolutely loved my trips there. But the insights didn't stop there. This past-life adventure became a lesson in karmic healing.

A month later, my husband and I went to visit Aunt Fay. When we arrived, she handed me a big box for my birthday. I was touched to find that it contained a piece of her blue and white porcelain that I had particularly liked—a teapot. Her unselfish generosity touched a sensitive chord deep within me. When my mother had died a couple of years before, I had honored Mom's wish to give something nice to each of the people close to her. However, I had been unwilling to give Mom's favorite piece of art to a particular woman in the family who wanted it. Although I gave her several other things, I knew in my heart that Mom would have given her the piece that she wanted. It still bothered me, but I rationalized.

The week after Aunt Fay gave me the teapot, I attended a birthday party for this relative. I wrapped the piece that I had withheld and gave it to her. Better late than never. Acts of kindness are truly like tossing pebbles into a pond. The ripples wash over us all and help us to be kind to others.

The Golden Key

Many years ago, Kathleen Horowitz, a longtime A.R.E. member and friend in Maryland, told me a very memorable story of being healed by using a spiritual exercise called "The Golden Key."[2] I never forgot her story, and as I was seeking stories for this book, I asked her to write it up for me.

Kathleen calls "The Golden Key" a practical recipe for getting out of trouble. In the foreword, author Emmet Fox writes that "study and research are well in their own time and place, but no amount of either will get you out of a concrete difficulty. Do exactly what 'The Golden Key' says, and if you are persistent you will overcome any difficulty."

The gift of this recipe came to Kathleen when a kind person saw her dissolve into tears at church. The choir had introduced a new song, "Be Not Afraid." But Kathleen *was* afraid. Less than ten hours earlier, she had left her husband, whom she deeply loved, because of physical abuse, and it felt as if her world had collapsed. The kind stranger said very little and just handed her the small booklet, which changed her life.

Kathleen's first "Golden Key" was a prayer to the Holy Spirit to come into her life. The booklet called this technique "scientific prayer." It explained that whether we pray or worry, we are creating and strengthening whatever we are concentrating on. As we replace worry with prayer, positive thoughts are sent from the mind and channeled over to the Divine. The power of the Golden Key is simply to stop thinking of the difficulty and think about God instead in the form of a positive belief statement.

This technique helped Kathleen dramatically over the next few months. It gave her something positive to do, rather than dwelling on her sorrow, and it was proactive. She felt that she could do something actively to create a better life. At first, she was Golden Keying about every fifteen seconds, then once a minute, then the time stretched out to once a day. She has since used the Golden Key to move through many subsequent problems, with equal assurance and success.

The Golden Key booklet brought Kathleen's childhood faith back to her. It was simple then, and it still is all these years later. The hardest part is just remembering to do it. Sometimes, when weeks pass and she is feeling anxious about some issue in her life, she suddenly surrenders, shakes her head, and says, "I should have been Golden Keying this." With that simple epiphany, her despair turns to expectation.

The Golden Key was also there for the *big* problems, such as when she was diagnosed with breast cancer. Her Golden Key was easy to remember and used with great frequency: "I can do all things through Christ who strengthens me." She was especially grateful because it enabled her to model a simple faith exercise for her children and husband. Again it was proactive; she expected to get better and she did. Her family also began to believe in the power of the Golden Key. If she had not recovered, Kathleen writes that she planned to be a model of dying well and doing so proactively.

The concept behind "The Golden Key" has been written about in many publications. It is not original or unique. Kathleen has collected many books that affirm the truth behind the concept, both spiritually and scientifically, but she knows that nothing replaces actually *doing it*. Kathleen summarizes her experience this way: "*Do* exactly what 'The Golden Key' says, and if you are persistent enough, you will overcome any difficulty. It is that simple. I promise."

It Is Done!

In closing this part of the book on transforming karma into grace, I want to end with a story that demonstrates the application of several spiritual principles. I met a very dynamic businesswoman named Kathy Lewis while touring with a group of A.R.E. members. Her success in receiving guidance and manifesting abundance impressed me. Kathy is the founder and president of the Capstone Institute of Mortgage Finance in Marietta, Georgia. She experienced so many miracles in both her business and personal life that, at the urging of her friends, she wrote a book about them, *It Is Done!*[3]

It all started at a low point in her life when Kathy tried talking to God. God answered Kathy and told her that she needed to take time to get to know Him. She began talking to God like a friend, and miracles began to occur. Her first miracle was getting her perfect house at exactly the price she could afford. Kathy came to recognize the power of using her mind positively in prayer and realized that prayer should not be supplication but an expression of gratitude.

Over the years, Kathy built a series of successful businesses. By integrating her inner spiritual work with her daily work in the business world, she realized that when she ran into a problem, she had two choices. As she puts it: "I can run around like crazy and worry myself sick, wondering what I'm going to do, then try to do it by myself, or I can ask God to help me, then let it go, and trust that He will handle it!"[4]

As Kathy discovered her oneness with God, she found freedom from fear. She learned that whenever she has a problem troubling her that she has been unable to solve, she can take it to God at night before going to bed: "Lord, I know there is a solution for this problem and I know You have the answer. Thank You, Lord, for bringing this answer to me."[5] Kathy has found that when she awakens the next morning, the answer always comes to her. And since the answer is from God, she knows it's always the right answer. However, Kathy is careful to say that this doesn't mean that we don't encounter obstacles in life. Since we are on Earth to learn and grow, obstacles allow us the opportunity to stretch to a higher level of accomplishment.

Through sharing her story with others over the years, Kathy encountered an important principle of doing spiritual work—the power of belief. She came to realize why more people don't experience miracles in their lives: "If they don't believe, they don't receive!"[6]

Despite asking for God's help, Kathy also strived to do her part. Very often in the process of dealing with a problem, she was led to the perfect solution in an improbable manner. For example, when money was tight because she was setting up a new office, she "affirmed" a new fax machine and thanked God for it. Less than a week later, a former student, who had never paid for his training class, called. Someone had given him a new fax machine that he didn't need, and he wanted to know if she would accept it as payment for the training course! This was just one of many such miraculous experiences.

Kathy's greatest joy has been sharing her miracles with her staff and helping them understand that God's miracles are also available to them if they will just ask. Through a miracle of acquiring inexpensive excess office space, in 2002 Kathy opened Capstone Spiritual Foundation, where she teaches classes on spiritual subjects.

Part IV:
Beyond Reincarnation—
Moving Into Other Dimensions

Quite an enviable position, may it be said, that the entity occupies; in the matter of truth, veracity, clean living, that the entity has made in this experience! and there will be little need, unless desired, for a return to this earth's experience.

For, there may be those cleansings that will make for, "Come thou and enjoy rather the glory of thy Lord, for it may be said thou hast truly shown that thou preferest thy brother to thine own gratification!"

322-2

14

Graduation From Earth School

For each cycle is as a grade in the experience of an entity or soul . . .
1703-3

Reincarnation Unnecessary

If there is kept that purpose in self, there is little need for a return;
save as one that may lead the way to those that are still in dark-
ness.   *1472-1*

Questions about reincarnation and karma cry out for answers. How do
we heal our karma and move forward? How do we end this seemingly
eternal cycle of reincarnation? How do we achieve the great escape and
graduate from Earth school? Cayce provided some answers to these questions.

Nearly two thousand people received life readings from Cayce between 1923 and 1944. Of these, only eighteen were told that they might
not have to reincarnate if they continued along their present path. The
choice would be up to them. They could move on to other "realms of
instruction" (5366-1), or they could return to Earth to work some more
and be of service to others. We will take a look at three of these unique
readings.

In 1979 Violet Shelley published a classic study of these cases called

177

Reincarnation Unnecessary.[1] Interestingly, she could find no single pattern that was shared by all of these eighteen people. Apparently, they were neither saintly nor perfect. This is a very hopeful sign for all of us who are still here.

Nero's Companion [5366]
Who would tell the rose how to be beautiful . . . ?   5366-1

Here is a very inspiring reading that offers hope to us all. In many respects, it is a testimony to the power of our free will. Less than two months before he gave his last reading, Edgar Cayce told a fifty-four-year-old woman that she had been Nero's companion. Despite this unpleasant piece of news, the Source went on to tell her that she had made such progress since that time that she may not need to reincarnate!

> This entity was among those with that one who persecuted the church so thoroughly and fiddled while Rome burned. That's the reason this entity in body has been disfigured by structural conditions. Yet may this entity be set apart. For through its experiences in the earth, it has advanced from a low degree to that which may not even necessitate a reincarnation in the earth. Not that it has reached perfection but there are realms for instruction if the entity will hold to that ideal of those whom it once scoffed at because of the pleasure materially brought in associations with those who did the persecuting.

However, the reading revealed that an Old Testament lifetime which preceded her Roman incarnation had provided bitter experiences for this soul:

> . . . the entity was in the land when the children of promise entered into the promised land, when [her] father [Achan] sought for the gratifying of selfish desires in gold and garments and in things which would gratify only the eye. The entity was young in years and yet felt, as from those things which were told the entity, that a lack of material consideration was given the parent.

This is a reference to a story in the seventh chapter of the Book of Joshua in which her father confessed to having stolen spoils of silver and gold from the Children of Israel. For this crime he was stoned to death, apparently in front of his family. Gladys Davis wrote about this in an early A.R.E. publication:

> Let's think a moment about the effect on this young girl. Not only was her mother widowed and all the children made fatherless, but for the rest of their lives they suffered shame and humiliation. At the time, the girl was very young and didn't fully understand why all this was happening; but later on when she was told about the reasons for her father's death sentence, she felt, the reading says, that he was unjustly put to death.
>
> **5366-1, R3**

It was this scarred and embittered soul who carried forward vengeful and destructive emotions into her next incarnation as a companion of Nero . . .

> . . . who persecuted those who believed in, those who accepted faith in righteousness, in goodness, in crucifying of body desires, in crucifying the emotions which would gratify only appetites of a body, either through the physical self or through physical appetites of gormandizing, and of material desire for the arousing more of the beast in individual souls.
>
> In the [present] experience, then, the entity is meeting self . . .

Gladys Davis continued with this soul's story:

> We can see how as the companion or associate of Nero she would have every opportunity to feel the emotion of "getting even" with those who had stoned her father. Perhaps some of the Christians being persecuted were reincarnated souls who had unmercifully stoned her father—or perhaps she had personally known them before the persecution and had hated them "without a cause" so far as could be judged in that lifetime. At any rate, as Nero's com-

panion, she participated in the persecutions.

The reading gives only one incarnation between her life with Nero and the present. She must have done a great deal of work in her previous life to have moved from her Roman excesses to her present possibility of earthly graduation.

> Before this we find the entity was in the land of the present nativity, through the experiences in seeking for new undertakings with the associates or companions. The entity became a helper to those who sought to know more of that which had been the prompting of individuals to seek freedom and to know that which is the spirit of creation or creative energies. Thus did the entity grow in attempting to interpret man's relationship to the Creative Forces or God.

Her previous life was also in America, where she apparently sought new opportunities and relationships with others (not presumably the Nero crowd). The reading states that she served other people in their seeking to understand freedom and their relationships to God.

Her reading ends with a beautiful passage for a beautiful soul:

> Who would tell the rose how to be beautiful; who would give to the morning sun, glory; who would tell the stars how to be beautiful? Keep that faith! which has prompted thee. Many will gain much from thy patience, thy consistence, thy brotherly love.

Remember that this reading began by saying, "That's the reason this entity in body has been disfigured by structural conditions." Here is the letter this woman wrote to Edgar when she requested her reading:

> I have lived most of my life by knowing the power of God would keep me alive and active. At present I am taking 12 sulfur baths and massage to try to get absolutely well. My troubles now are: Right ear and Eustachian tube collapsed. Lower colon stretched very large and small passage. Tired all the time. Use of arms

slows my heart and I become exhausted standing on my feet very long. Also cannot sit down very long. Nerves down my legs hurt and pain when I lie on them or stand. Why should I come into this life with such a broken physical body? It seems I have been through hell, but an interesting trip so far, and I have often wondered what I have saved myself for. Have always wanted to be a service to humanity but no strength—angina—pernicious anemia, etc., and so on since I was young. Have I committed a great crime (murder) in the past or now—?

Ironically, she wonders if she has committed murder in the past. This thought, of course, is close to the truth; she was a companion to one of the most notorious and heartless murderers in history. Yet, despite her overwhelming physical suffering, which she refers to as "hell," she is able to jest that it has been "an interesting trip." Very tellingly, she also says that she has always wanted to be of service to humanity. Furthermore, her letter starts right off by stating her faith in God.

In a letter written in 1948, she included a follow-up report on her reading that contains a humorous anecdote, supporting the veracity of the reading:

When (I was) young, my mother wanted me to take music lessons because she received much satisfaction playing by ear and I had no talent. At the end of a term the music teacher dismissed me as a disgrace to her teaching. I learned quickly and easily "The Ben Hur Chariot Race." Played it on all occasions so fast and dramatically that it shocked all listeners. When I looked at the picture on the outside of the sheet, the charging steeds and chariots racing with the Roman Arena filled with cheering crowds I became as one with the whole living action, was aware of nothing until I hit the final note. At 57 I think I could still play parts of it although I have not touched a piano for over 40 years. (It was the only piece I could play.)

Her report conveyed the attitude with which she had faced her suffering. But it also showed the dramatic improvement in her health.

> When in grade school and on through college we never knew if
> I would live, was given up to die several times but by will power
> I struggled on, never complaining but in constant pain. Medi-
> cine always seemed to make me worse. Now I am almost the
> picture of health and younger looking than when twenty.

This report closed with a resounding affirmation of the reading she
received from Edgar Cayce. We can also glimpse some of her qualities of
spirit that doubtlessly contributed to her potential graduation from
Earth school:

> The reading has been a godsend in helping me to understand
> the whys of my struggle to exist physically and mentally. My
> dear mother used to say "You must be saved for a purpose." My
> brother, M.D. specialist, said: "Nothing seems to help you; if you
> live it will be because you experiment upon yourself."
>
> Near death I heard "iodine for leukemia" three nights in
> succession and it pleased me to read how much you have
> recommended it. Have always hoped I would never have to live
> again . . . I still have much to overcome.

Nero Himself [33]
> *See, this is Nero.*   *33-1*

It would be hard to find two people whose attitudes toward their
suffering differed more dramatically than Nero and his former companion. In July 1926, Mr. Cayce received a letter requesting a reading
from a twenty-four-year-old ex-coal miner in West Virginia.

> I was hurt in a car wreck 4 years ago . . . I am paralyzed from my
> neck down. I have been operated on 3 times but all the doctors
> don't seem to find what's the matter with me.   **33-1, R2**

Cayce gave him a physical reading on August 31. It began by saying
that a life reading for this man would be of more interest than a physical reading. And, while some relief could be found, little could be done
without a very great deal of effort to restore normal function. Appar-

ently, many of his problems were merited by a past life which so over-shadowed his present life that the Source chose to very quietly volunteer a startling piece of information. Gladys later noted in this reading report that it was given "in an undertone so that we could hardly hear it."

> Now, the experience of this entity through this present physical plane, as a developing entity through earth's experiences would be more interesting than the physical conditions, for these are of the nature that, while assistance and relief may be brought, there is little to be done to bring the normal forces of the body, save through untiring energy, trouble, patience, and persistence . . .
>
> Keep the whole mentality in that way as to build the best development, for, as has been seen, many of these conditions are merited through those actions of the mental forces and the spiritual forces of the body. . . See, this is Nero. We are through for the present.   33-1

Gladys reported that they did not include this startling revelation in the copy of the reading that was sent to the man. In 1928 "Nero" wrote the following to Edgar Cayce:

> I rec'd a letter telling me you have your hospital fixed ready . . . if you say you can cure me, I will give you $1,000, and if you don't you won't get anything. Isn't that fair?   33-1, R2

In a letter to Morton Blumenthal (excerpts of which were contained in this same report), Edgar later offered these thoughts about "Nero":

> This man received . . . an accident to his physical being, that has made him a helpless invalid . . . [and] he appealed to us for help. We haven't been able to do any good, from the physical standpoint. [Y]et the information . . . supplied to that man, illiterate as he may be considered by others, has been able to awaken in him something of a spiritual understanding . . . [and he] becomes aware of the destructive forces meted out to him through destruc-

tion he wrought on mankind at another period of his existence in
the earth plane . . . [H]e now finds himself face to face with
himself, and with [what] he has created by the actions of his
physical self . . . without respect to his soul . . . and now the whole
being cries out for succor and aid!   900-295, R1

A letter sent to this man in 1940 came back marked "Deceased." Gladys
later offered the final hopeful summation of "Nero's" karma:

**For 18 years he was completely helpless and thus entirely
dependent upon charitable Christians for every detail of his
care. This experience enabled him to meet and overcome much
of the bad karma resulting from his Nero reign.   33-1, R2**

A Very Handicapped Child [4502]
As ye would that men should do unto you, do ye even so to them.
Matthew 7:12

Here is another very unusual case from the *Reincarnation Unnecessary*
readings. It is the first one ever given, just three months after Lammer's
groundbreaking past-life reading in October 1923. However, the reference to the child's not having to return may well have been overlooked.
In addition, of the eighteen such readings, this is the only one that was
definite; it states that the soul "will" (not may) build to the point of not
needing to return. It is also the only physical (not life) reading in which
Cayce said that a soul need not return.

The subject is a very handicapped one-year-old child. His aunt wrote
to Cayce, requesting the reading on January 23, 1924. "He's lived with
me since the death of his mother; he can't ask for a reading and
never will unless a change; he's been afflicted since birth." (4502-1, B1)
The reading said in part:

Now in this body we will find those conditions that would be
an interesting study psychologically, pathologically or biologi-
cally . . .

This body, in the physical, may be assisted, yet never given the
full perfect control of all of the portions of the system; yet the soul

and spirit force . . . will build to the developing upon this plane towards that point from which every soul and spirit force takes its flight, and to which purpose all individual entities are entered into the earth plane.

In the physical we find that lack of coordination in the system, that allows the physical to become a taxation to soul and spirit entity . . .

Care, persistence and attention must be given at all times. It is worth the price to any that would accomplish these. See that they are thoroughly carried forth, for in this we will see the manifestations of that injunction "As ye would that men should do unto you, do ye even so to them."   4502-1

The reading states that complete physical healing for this child is not possible. Cayce did give suggestions to provide some physical relief. However, this soul, so very taxed by ill health, is told that it will build toward the star Arcturus, through which graduating souls exit our solar system. This reading demonstrates very well that we cannot judge spiritual development by external appearances. It ends by giving very serious guidance to the child's caregivers. The dedicated care that the little boy required offered a great spiritual growth opportunity to anyone who provided it. If diligent, the caregivers would do no less than learn to manifest the golden rule.

Gladys updated this file in 1983: "We never heard further from the aunt regarding this case. It is safe to assume that the reading was not understood or followed. No contribution was made to Mr. Cayce; the reading was gratis." (4502-1, R1)

I'm sure that Edgar didn't mind not being paid for helping this suffering but beautiful soul.

Love Is Giving

Law is love. Love is giving. Giving is as God, the Maker.   **3744-2**

In her classic work, Violet Shelley looked for common patterns among this group of special graduates. In terms of past lives or astrological influences, she found none. What she did find, however, applies

to us all. It is the key to healing our karma. It is the heart of the great
commandment. It is that little but very big word—love. These eighteen
unique readings contain assessments like these:

> . . . for those that seek *through* love will find.   560-1

> One that may give much joy to many peoples, always giving,
> giving, more than ever receiving.   569-6

> . . . the entity has in . . . most of its sojourns [in] the earth *given—*
> *given—given* of self . . .   1143-2

> . . . we find that desire ever is shown in the entity to give of the
> best, and not reserving self in any manner.   2903-1

> . . . in those experiences when self lost self—as it were—in that
> it gave to others, in the character of . . . losing of self in service to
> others . . .   444-1

> One who gives . . . [to] others often in preference [to] self . . .
>   . . . bringing joy, peace, happiness, to many, and in . . . [a] . . .
> position of a . . . .life well spent, even in luxury—though never
> abusing same, for the entity gave—gave—gave—to others, in
> word, deed . . .   4500-1

> . . . in each of those experiences self-aggrandizement has never
> been a fault, and [it is] hard for the entity to understand an
> individual that is so warped in self as to set selfish interests before
> that of its fellow man.   2504-4

> . . . only as an individual gives itself in service does it become
> aware. For as the divine love [is] manifested . . . that alone ye have
> given away do ye possess. That *alone* is the manner in which the
> growth, the awareness, the consciousness grows to be.
>   For until the experiences are thine, thy awareness cannot be
> complete.   1472-1

> . . . the conquering of self is truly greater than were one to
> conquer *many* worlds . . .   115-1

In a reading for a couple planning to get married, Cayce gave my
favorite description of love. I read this passage during the wedding cer-
emony of some dear friends:

> Remember each, love is giving; it is a growth. It may be cultivated
> or it may be seared. That of selflessness on the part of each is
> necessary . . . Love grows; love endures; love forgiveth; love
> understands; love keeps those things rather as opportunities that
> to others would become hardships.   939-1

So whether you're getting married or trying to graduate from this
Earth, we all need to always remember these wise words: "Love is giving."

15

Star Gate Arcturus

For, the earth is only an atom in the universe of worlds!   5749-3

At this point in our study of the soul's cosmic journey, at least two major questions naturally arise: First, after we graduate from this solar system, where do we go next? Second, how do we get there? To answer the second question first, how we graduate from Earth and move on is really the subject of this book—reincarnation and karma. This process is our pathway to spiritual progress—practice makes perfect. Answering the first question involves taking a look at another unique concept from the Cayce readings. The very few readings regarding where we go next tell us that after leaving this solar system, our souls go to a great star called Arcturus. These readings give us a fascinating peek into another dimension.

Cayce's source describes Arcturus in a couple of different ways:

Arcturus . . . is the way, is the door out of this system.   2454-3

[the] realm . . . of Arcturus [is] that center from which there may

be the entrance into other realms of consciousness . . . 2823-1

. . . Arcturus is that which may be called the center of this universe, through which individuals pass and at which period there comes the choice of the individual as to whether it is to return to complete there—that is, in this planetary system, our sun, the earth sun and its planetary system—or to pass on to others. . .   5749-14

It sounds rather like graduate school. After university graduation, we can go somewhere else for higher studies or we can stay where we are and work and study more. Again, it's a matter of our individual free will.

Four Who Returned From Arcturus

As to the appearances—these are so varied, as may be indicated from the entity's appearance in the earth from Arcturus . . .
                                                              2454-3

Out of the two thousand life readings, only three women and one man were told that they had gone to Arcturus but had chosen to return to Earth rather than go on to other realms. All four were told that their choice to return to Earth was of their own free will and that their decisions had been made "purposefully" or for a "definite mission." However, their readings never explained their purpose or mission any further. All four were interested in things of a mystical nature. And, for whatever reason, the three women had their readings very late in Edgar's life.

Edgar himself was the fourth person and only man, according to the readings, who had attained the growth necessary to proceed to Arcturus, after a lifetime as an Egyptian priest twelve thousand years ago. However, when he chose to return to Earth, he made choices and incurred karma that necessitated painful lessons through several additional incarnations.

Obviously, there are no guarantees when we use our free will. That greatest of gifts is also a very great responsibility. We must always seek to use this freedom wisely. However, since all four of these returnees chose not to go on but to go back to Earth, we can see that even in the realms of Arcturus, our God–given free will is still completely free. The choice was still theirs.

One of the three women who returned to Earth from Arcturus wrote a letter to Edgar seeking clarification about Arcturus. The waking Cayce wrote back, answering her inquiry this way:

> . . . you have a wonderful reading . . . true [it] seems there is a good deal expected of you this time, but you are capable of meeting it. You like all of us have your problems, but are we all as well qualified to meet them?
>
> Arcturus—from the information is the means of one passing from this immediate solar system—and those who return from same—do so of their own purpose, for some definite purpose in the Earth—hence those of whom much is expected—happen to be one of those myself, have had very few of them through the years of experience with such information—only three as I recall just now but may have been more—each are in the position that others look to them for guidance often.   2454-3, R2

This woman was Eula Allen, teacher and author of a wonderful trilogy of books about physical and spiritual creation based on the Cayce readings. In explaining that a few unique souls do volunteer to return to Earth to serve humanity, Cayce was supporting the Buddhist concept of Bodhisattvas.

Some Implications of Arcturus

> *. . . the soul of man . . . encompasses all in this solar system or in others.*   5755-2

In 1941, as he was working on the manuscript for *There Is a River*, Tom Sugrue asked Cayce about Arcturus.

> (Q) . . . [i]t was given through this source that the entity Edgar Cayce . . . went to the system of Arcturus, and then returned to earth. Does this indicate a usual or an unusual step in soul evolution?

(A) . . . [t]his was an unusual step, and yet a usual one.

5749-14

Regarding Edgar's return from Arcturus, the Source calls it an unusual yet a usual step. If we look at the statistics from the readings, clearly it is an unusual step in that only four out of two thousand people who received life readings attained that level. However, given our spiritual destiny as souls, it becomes a usual step, since we will all attain Arcturus when we have earned that privilege.

Sugrue continued asking his deep questions about the implications of the role of Arcturus:

(Q) . . . [i]s it necessary to finish the solar system cycle before going to other systems?

(A) Necessary to finish the solar cycle.

(Q) Can oneness be attained — or the finish of evolution reached — on any system, or must it be in a particular one?

(A) Depending upon what system the entity has entered, to be sure. It may be completed in any of the many systems.

(Q) Must the solar cycle be finished on earth, or can it be completed on another planet, or does each planet have a cycle of its own which must be finished?

(A) If it is begun on the earth it must be finished on the earth. The solar system of which the earth is a part is only a portion of the whole . . . It is the cycle of the whole system that is finished, see? . . .

(Q) Do souls become entangled in other systems as they did in this system?

(A) In other systems that represent the same as the earth does in this system, yes.   5749-14

As if living many lives in the Earth were not enough, Cayce's readings opened up an even more staggering vision of our cosmic journey and our destiny as souls. Our solar system is not the only school system there is! Cayce says there are many other systems. However, if we incarnate here, we must finish our course work here, before moving on to another, higher school system elsewhere in the universe. Apparently, in the distant past, other souls made poor choices as we did, incurred karma as we did, and are working it out as we are in other planetary systems somewhere in space.

A follow-up reading to this fascinating information on other systems was given a month later:

(Q) May we assume that the term "entangle" means a soul's participation and immersion in a form or system . . . which was not necessarily intended for such . . . as the earth?

(A) To be sure . . . the earth is that speck, that part of creation where souls projected themselves into matter, and thus brought that conscious awareness of the ability of creating without those forces of the spirit of truth. . .

As this came about, it was necessary for their own awareness . . . Thus realms of systems came into being . . .

(Q) In systems where conditions for expression parallel those in the solar system; is entanglement a parallel experience to entanglement in this system, so that a soul is apt only to become immersed in one of these systems, and after working out of it, be immune to the attractions of others?

(A) No. No two leaves of a tree are the same. No two blades of grass are the same. No two systems have the same awareness, neither are they parallel . . . But canst thou conceive—the requirements . . . to meet all the idiosyncrasies of a *single* soul? How many systems would it require? . . . Yet all are the work of His hand, are thine to possess, thine to use . . .

(Q) Can you describe . . . what it is in other systems which attracts the souls?

(A) . . . there are conditions that may meet every idiosyncrasy of the *individual* soul! Then consider the millions . . . Is God's hand short, that there would not be all that each soul would require? For it is not by the will of God that any soul perishes, but with every temptation, with every trial there is prepared the way of escape. . .

(Q) Do these other systems have a planet, like earth, which is a

focal point for the meeting and material expression of its forces
and principles?
(A) Relatively so, in that dimension of consciousness or awareness
necessary to meet that arousing of the soul to its . . . awareness of
the Maker . . .

   For, an individual soul here finds itself a body, a mind, a soul.
Ye may sin in mind, ye may sin in body. Do ye answer only in
spirit?

   As He has given, every *soul* shall give account of the deeds
done in the body. What body? That body of mind, that body of
physical manifestation, that body of spirit; each in its own sphere,
its own realm.   5755-2

This follow-up reading explains why the vast realms of celestial systems came into being. Once we chose to become involved in the Earth
and lost our spiritual consciousness, God made "the universe of worlds"
for us—for our growth and our salvation—that we may return to Him.
No two systems are the same. Just like on Earth—given our free will,
even as we progress—we can always fall again. It is beyond comprehension to imagine that there are worlds to meet all of the idiosyncrasies of
each and every soul! No matter the individual soul's circumstances,
there is always a path of progress. Given the universal law of karma, we
meet our sins at the same level at which we created them—physically,
mentally, and spiritually. Therefore, other systems, too, have a planet for
material expression, like our Earth.

Clearly, we are not alone. Countless soul-development dramas are
playing out across the universe. The scope of this amazing, unseen,
spiritual evolution is far beyond anything that we can conceive of with
our three-dimensional minds or even imagine. God gives us all many,
many opportunities to grow. Thankfully, because of who we really are—
spiritual beings—the final outcome is not in doubt. As we take the higher
karmic road and choose aright, we will all eventually go home.

   . . . though there may be worlds, many universes, even much as
   to solar systems, greater than our own that we enjoy in the present,
   this earthly experience on this earth is a mere speck when

> considered even with our own solar system. Yet the soul of man,
> thy soul, encompasses *all* in this solar system or in others.
>
> 5755-2

We are star people—citizens of eternity!

Arcturus According to Astronomy

Since I found Cayce's information on Arcturus so fascinating, I wanted to see what science says about our soul's cosmic escape hatch. Arcturus is a giant star that shines over one hundred times brighter than our sun. Indeed, astronomy tells us that Arcturus is the brightest star in the northern hemisphere and the fourth brightest star in the entire sky. It is thirty-seven light years away and shines with a soft orange light from the constellation of the Great Bear, Bootes. The surface temperature on Arcturus is approximately 4000° Celsius.

Arcturus became well known when its light was used to open the Chicago World's Fair in 1933, because that light had left Arcturus at approximately the time of the previous Chicago World's Fair in 1893.[1] Our souls certainly graduate through a very impressive heavenly body.

16

The Bottom Line–
Some Concluding Thoughts

All *things are possible with God.*   *971-1*

The Good News Is That There Is Only Good News

Ye are *indeed gods in the making!*   *816-3*

So what's the bottom line in Cayce's saga of reincarnation and karma? Let's conclude with a few powerful thoughts to keep in mind. These ideas will help us stay positive as we move on through our spiritual journey.

I like the way Herb Puryear, a former A.R.E. staff member, summed it all up, "The good news is that there is only good news because God is love." Essentially, this view sums up the Cayce philosophy. Pain is temporary; love is eternal.

> When all about you seems disturbed, when all seems lost, know
> that He in His love, and in His patience, can turn such conditions
> into victorious joy, into gladness that makes the heart, the mind,
> the eyes, the body, the voice, joyous in living for the Christ's sake.
>   3165-1

Cayce tells us that we can move from all seeming lost to victorious joy. The news can't get any better than that.

Reincarnation—Life is a Gift

For . . . heaven and hell is built by the soul!   **5753-1**

Reincarnation is just a part of the continuity of life. Life never ends; we just change form. Cayce puts it this way:

> Because an atom . . . matter, a form, is changed does not mean that the essence, the source or the spirit has changed; only in its form of manifestation, and *not* in its relation [to God]. 5753-1

In essence, reincarnation is about who we are, that is, who we *really* are in the very core of our being. Each of us is a child of God, and Genesis 1: 26–27 tells us twice that we are made in His image. God does not die and neither do we. Life is like energy: it is indestructible. Essentially, life is spirit—and spirit cannot be destroyed. It only changes form, sometimes visible, sometimes invisible to our physical eyes. The Cayce readings say that a soul is composed of spirit, mind, and will. This is who we really are. The Spirit of our Creator is our spark of life. Our miraculous minds span both the physical and the spiritual realms and record all of our experiences. And we are the only creatures within creation to be gifted with entirely free will. Of course, we must always meet the consequences of our choices, both positive and negative.

We are unique in creation, capable of becoming godlike: "For *only* in man is there the existence of the soul that is not just universal, but individual; capable of becoming as a god, as one with the Creative Forces." (487-17) The scope of our souls is beyond comprehension.

In response to a deep question framed by Tom Sugrue, Cayce's source further defined our essence and told us who we are at our deepest level.

> (Q) Should the Christ-Consciousness be described as the aware-ness within each soul, imprinted in pattern on the mind and waiting to be awakened by the will, of the soul's oneness with God?

(A) Correct. That's the idea exactly!   5749-14

Cayce defines the Christ Consciousness as "a universal consciousness of the Father Spirit" (5749-4) and "the love of God Consciousness." (281-13) He uses the term in a universal, not a religious or sectarian, fashion. Thus, as so many holy sources tell us, we are souls, one with our Maker and made in the image of the Highest. That pattern is within our minds, which partakes of both the spiritual and physical realms. It only awaits activation by the power of the choices that we make and through which we may come to know our oneness with our Creator! That, according to the Cayce readings, is who we really are.

Always remember that understanding who we are is the key to understanding reincarnation and karma. Cayce uses a wonderful term to describe us—*co-creators*. God created us to be co-creators with Him. It is staggering to try to imagine what that means. There is no higher potential, no higher attainment. We are truly limitless beings. Think about our concept of God—omnipotent and omniscient—all-powerful and all-knowing. We, too, are potentially omnipotent and omniscient.

I often think that the world is so messy because we really don't know who we are; otherwise we wouldn't behave the way we do. But we do get all the opportunities we need to work it out. We have been on a very long journey, but we can change course whenever we want to. It's all up to us!

(Q) Can I finish my purpose in this incarnation, so that I will not need to return to the earth?
(A) As may any; if they will but put *off* the old and on the new— that is in Him; becoming aware of that *I Am* conscience within self that becomes one with Him. Yes.
(Q) And how long will I have to do this?
(A) How long will you require?   1037-1

All Karma Is Good Karma

Though He were the Son, yet learned He obedience through the things which He suffered.   3143-1

I began this book by using one of my favorite quotes from the cartoon character Pogo: "We have met the enemy and he is us." Pogo said it all. We have no one to blame and no one to thank for our present circumstances but ourselves. Karma is from us to us. However, our cosmic journey is all about learning, and we are always learning even when we resist, perhaps most of all when we resist. The learning mechanism is the ever-present law of karma—simply cause and effect. Cayce warns us that "there is the continual warring of flesh, or materiality, with the spiritual influences." (69-4). When we knock our heads against a brick wall, at some point it sinks in—this is not working, this does not feel good. This is all part of our soul's evolutionary odyssey. It is spiritual education. Thus all karma is good karma because it makes us face ourselves; it forces us to make choices; it stretches us to grow; it propels us toward our spiritual destiny.

Understanding that karma is a neutral law, simply a mechanism of cause and effect, is empowering. We are in the driver's seat. We are in control. If we want golden karma, all we need to do is practice the golden rule. This is another way of saying love is giving, and giving is how the eighteen Earth graduates made it to Arcturus. If we use our minds and wills positively, we will build positive karma and a positive future. It truly is that simple. Thus we are all spiritual alchemists, healing our karma and transforming it into the grace of God.

> For Life *is*, and it is earnest, and it is good, and it is sad, and it *is* beautiful, and it is ugly; just as ye apply it in thy dealings and relations with thy fellow man—as patterned from thy ideal.
>
> Then indeed it is what it is in the present because of what ye have set in motion or done about same in thy experiences here, now, and *throughout* the ages of thy sojourn in the earth as well as in the interims about the environs of the earth between the earthly sojourns.   1551-2

Karmically, we are the sum of all we've ever chosen to do. This is a very sobering thought. We are each right where we belong, right where we have placed ourselves. And this place is the perfect place for us to learn our lessons—right here, right now. However, none of this changes who we are at our deepest level. We remain souls made in His image; we have the pattern of the universal consciousness of God within us. Thus the deck is stacked in our favor. All we need to do is call upon our own divine nature. If we truly want to do this, we cannot fail. *It is who we really are!*

Cayce makes it very clear that we merit our problems because we have built them. They are our very personal responsibilities, which we cannot avoid confronting. Problems are also good karma because they are opportunities that we tailored to ourselves, and they fit our own specific growth needs. As I have learned, stubborn problems such as incurable, hereditary illnesses require constant and persistent work. This does not mean that we can't enjoy life. One of the keys to healing bodily karma is balance and purpose: "Budget thy time as to play, as to work, as to recreation, as to pleasure, as to improving body, improving mind, yea in finding thy purpose in spirit and in truth." (3659-1) The other key is purpose. Cayce often asked people why they wanted to get well. What was their purpose? Was it to be able to go right back to the bad habits that made them sick to begin with?

Illness is a wake-up call. A failed relationship is also a wake-up call. We must take personal responsibility for our problems. How many times will we hide from life—just hit the snooze alarm button and pull the covers over our heads?

> For He hath not willed that a soul should perish, but has with each temptation, each experience, prepared that way in which that experience, of whatever nature it may be, may be a helpful one for the entity—if the entity will but look to Him as the giver and the author of life, and of all that makes for harmony and peace within the experience of a soul. 1966-1

Often when people see all the suffering in the world, they ask why a loving God allows these things to happen. One of the great strengths of the philosophy of reincarnation is that it explains ultimate justice. We realize that it is the impersonal law of cause and effect which accounts for illness, poverty, and suffering in the world. It is not God's doing; we do it to ourselves. So the good news of reincarnation is that it allows us additional opportunities to improve. And the good news of karma is that all karma is good karma because a loving God wouldn't have it any other way!

Notes

Chapter One
1. Glenn Sanderfur, *Lives of the Master* (Virginia Beach, Virginia: A.R.E. Press, 1988), p. 24.

Chapter Five
1. *The Random House Unabridged Dictionary of the English Language* (New York, Random House, Inc., 1966), p. 165.
2. Joseph Head and S.L. Cranston, *Reincarnation: The Phoenix Fire Mystery*: (New York: Crown Publishers, Inc., 1977), p. 12.
3. *The Random House Unabridged Dictionary of the English Language* (New York, Random House, Inc., 1966), p. 165.

Chapter Six
1. Gina Cerminara, *Many Mansions* (New York: New American Library, Inc., 1950), pp. 47–53.

Chapter Eight
1. Linda Schiller–Hanna is a professional clairvoyant living in Ohio. Her Web site is www.lightworker22.com.
2. Dr. Joan Hanley is an A.R.E. member, retired elementary school principal, and longtime Atlantis enthusiast. Joan has led many research and tour groups to Bimini, and lives in Florida.

Chapter Nine
1. http://www.loyno.edu/~seduffy/mongols.html.

Chapter Ten
1. *Webster's New Collegiate Dictionary* (Springfield, Massachusetts: G & C Merriam Company, 1979), p. 494.

Chapter Eleven
1. *Webster's New Collegiate Dictionary* (Springfield, Massachusetts, G. & C. Merriam Company, 1979), p. 563.

Chapter Thirteen
1. *A Search for God*, Book I (Virginia Beach, Virginia: A.R.E. Press, 1970), p. 6.
2. Emmet Fox, *The Golden Key* (Unity Village, Missouri: Unity School of Christianity, 1931), p. 3.
3. Kathy Lewis, *It Is Done!* (Marietta, Georgia: N2Print, 2002).
4. Ibid, p. 20.
5. Ibid, p. 30.
6. Ibid, p. 40.

Chapter Fourteen
1. An analysis of all eighteen readings can be found in Violet Shelley's absorbing book, *Reincarnation Unnecessary*, published by A.R.E. Press, 1979.

Chapter Fifteen
1. www.astro.uicu.edu written by Jim Kaler.

References and Recommended Reading

A Search for God, Book I and Book II. Virginia Beach, Virginia: A.R.E. Press, 1970.

Cayce, Edgar. *Reincarnation and Karma*. (Edited by John Van Auken) Virginia Beach, Virginia: A.R.E. Press, 2006.

Cerminara, Gina. *Many Mansions*. New York: New American Library, Inc., 1950.

Cerminara, Gina. *Many Mansions, Part II*. Virginia Beach, Virginia: A.R.E. Press, 1985.

Church, W.H. *Many Happy Returns: The Lives of Edgar Cayce*. San Francisco: Harper & Row, 1984.

Daily, Dick. *The Edgar Cayce Bible Companion*. Virginia Beach, Virginia: A.R.E. Press, 1998.

Drummond, Richard H. *Unto the Churches*. Virginia Beach, Virginia: A.R.E. Press, 1978.

Fox, Emmet. *The Golden Key*. Unity Village, Missouri: Unity School of Christianity, 1931.

Frejer, B. Ernest. *The Edgar Cayce Companion*. Virginia Beach, Virginia: A.R.E. Press, 1995.

Gammon, Margaret H. *Astrology and the Edgar Cayce Readings*. Virginia Beach, Virginia: A.R.E. Press, 1974.

Grant, Robert J. *Universe of Worlds*. Virginia Beach, Virginia: A.R.E. Press, 2003.

Head, Joseph and S.L. Cranston. *Reincarnation: The Phoenix Fire Mystery*. New York: Crown Publishers, 1977.

The Holy Bible, King James Version.

The Holy Bible, New King James Version, 1982.

Kirkpatrick, Sidney. *Edgar Cayce: An American Prophet*. New York: Riverhead Books, 2000.

Langley, Noel. *Edgar Cayce on Reincarnation*. New York: Paperback Library, Inc., 1967.

Lewis, Kathy. *It Is Done!* Marietta, Georgia: N2Print, 2002.

Sanderfur, Glenn. *Lives of the Master*. Virginia Beach, Virginia: A.R.E. Press, 1988.

Shelley, Violet M. *Reincarnation Unnecessary*. Virginia Beach, Virginia: A.R.E. Press, 1979.

Smith, A. Robert. *No Soul Left Behind*. New York: Citadel Press Books, 2005.

Smith, Robert C. *Edgar Cayce: You Can Remember Your Past Lives*. New York: Warner Books, 1989.

Soul Development. Virginia Beach, Virginia: A.R.E. Press, 1986.

Sparrow, Lynn Elwell. *Reincarnation: Claiming Your Past, Creating Your Future*. New York: St. Martin's Press, 1988.

Sugrue, Thomas. *There Is a River*. Virginia Beach, Virginia: A.R.E. Press, 1997.

Thurston, Mark. *The Great Teachings of Edgar Cayce*. Virginia Beach, Virginia: A.R.E. Press, 1996.

Thurston, Mark. *More Great Teachings of Edgar Cayce*. Virginia Beach, Virginia: A.R.E. Press, 1997.

Todeschi, Kevin. *Family Karma*. Virginia Beach, Virginia: A.R.E. Press, 2005.

Todeschi, Kevin. *Reincarnation of Biblical Figures*. Virginia Beach, Virginia: A.R.E. Press, 1999.

Van Auken, John. *A.R.E.'s Personal Spirituality* Newsletters. Virginia Beach, Virginia.

Van Auken, John. *Born Again & Again*. Virginia Beach, Virginia: Inner Vision Publishing Co., 1989.

Van Auken, John. *Edgar Cayce on the Revelation*. Virginia Beach, Virginia: A.R.E. Press, 2000.

Van Auken, John. *Living in the Light* Newsletters. Virginia Beach, Virginia.

Van Auken, John. *Past Lives*. Virginia Beach, Virginia: Inner Vision Publishing Co., 1985.

Van Auken, John. *Reincarnation—Your Secret Life*. New York: Ballantine Books, 1991.

Woodward, Mary Anne. *Edgar Cayce's Story of Karma*. New York: Berkley Medallion Books, 1971.

Woodward, Mary Anne. *Scars of the Soul*. Fair Grove, Missouri: Brindabella Books, 1985.

EDGAR CAYCE'S A.R.E.

What Is A.R.E.?

The Association for Research and Enlightenment, Inc., (A.R.E.®) was founded in 1931 to research and make available information on psychic development, dreams, holistic health, meditation, and life after death. As an open-membership research organization, the A.R.E. continues to study and publish such information, to initiate research, and to promote conferences, distance learning, and regional events. Edgar Cayce, the most documented psychic of our time, was the moving force in the establishment of A.R.E.

Who Was Edgar Cayce?

Edgar Cayce (1877–1945) was born on a farm near Hopkinsville, Ky. He was an average individual in most respects. Yet, throughout his life, he manifested one of the most remarkable psychic talents of all time. As a young man, he found that he was able to enter into a self-induced trance state, which enabled him to place his mind in contact with an unlimited source of information. While asleep, he could answer questions or give accurate discourses on any topic. These discourses, more than 14,000 in number, were transcribed as he spoke and are called "readings."

Given the name and location of an individual anywhere in the world, he could correctly describe a person's condition and outline a regimen of treatment. The consistent accuracy of his diagnoses and the effectiveness of the treatments he prescribed made him a medical phenomenon, and he came to be called the "father of holistic medicine."

Eventually, the scope of Cayce's readings expanded to include such subjects as world religions, philosophy, psychology, parapsychology, dreams, history, the missing years of Jesus, ancient civilizations, soul growth, psychic development, prophecy, and reincarnation.

A.R.E. Membership

People from all walks of life have discovered meaningful and life-transforming insights through membership in A.R.E. To learn more about Edgar Cayce's A.R.E. and how membership in the A.R.E. can enhance your life, visit our Web site at EdgarCayce.org, or call us toll-free at 800-333-4499.

Edgar Cayce's A.R.E.
215 67th Street
Virginia Beach, VA 23451–2061

EDGARCAYCE.ORG